FREE SPEECH
ALL THAT MATTERS

About the author

Alan Haworth is a philosopher. As a university lecturer, he developed and taught courses in Ethics, Political Philosophy, and the History of Ideas. He is the author of numerous articles and several books. These include a critique of free market economic theory, an earlier book on free speech – now recognized as a standard text on the subject – and an acclaimed critical history of political philosophy, now in its second edition.

He has a reputation for his ability to explain difficult ideas with clarity.

Political Philosophy is, he says, the analysis and evaluation of arguments, their structure and the assumptions upon which they rest. The point is to understand their true practical significance, and, in the case of free speech, that significance is huge. Accordingly, in *Free Speech: All that Matters*, he sets out to take a step back and cast a cool eye over the main arguments surrounding that idea, or, to put it another way, to cast some light into a terrain which has become clouded by emotion, exaggeration and half-truth.

Otherwise, he is hardly unusual. He likes music, especially jazz, blues and Bach, he enjoys learning foreign languages, and he likes to travel. He lives in North London.

FREE SPEECH

Alan Haworth

ALL THAT MATTERS

First published in Great Britain in 2015 by Hodder and Stoughton. An Hachette UK company.

This edition published in 2015 by John Murray Learning

British Library Cataloguing in Publication Data: a catalogue record for this title is available from the British Library.

ISBN: 9781473602816

eISBN: 9781473602830

1

The publisher has used its best endeavours to ensure that any website addresses referred to in this book are correct and active at the time of going to press. However, the publisher and the author have no responsibility for the websites and can make no guarantee that a site will remain live or that the content will remain relevant, decent or appropriate.

The publisher has made every effort to mark as such all words which it believes to be trademarks. The publisher should also like to make it clear that the presence of a word in the book, whether marked or unmarked, in no way affects its legal status as a trademark.

Every reasonable effort has been made by the publisher to trace the copyright holders of material in this book. Any errors or omissions should be notified in writing to the publisher, who will endeavour to rectify the situation for any reprints and future editions.

Cover image © [cover image credit line to be inserted here]

Typeset by Cenveo® Publisher Services.

Printed and bound in Great Britain by CPI Group (UK) Ltd., Croydon, CR0 4YY.

John Murray Learning policy is to use papers that are natural, renewable and recyclable products and made from wood grown in sustainable forests. The logging and manufacturing processes are expected to conform to the environmental regulations of the country of origin.

Carmelite House
50 Victoria Embankment
London EC4Y 0DZ
www.hodder.co.uk

For Rowan

Contents

Acknowledgments

For encouraging me to write the book in the first place: George Miller

For their comments on an earlier draft: Alex Brown, John Charvet, Kai Spiekermann, Nigel Warburton

For their invaluable assistance with the '100 ideas' section: Julian Baggini, Rowan Dawkins, Timothy Garton Ash, Matt Haworth, Sue Lamble

Picture Credits

OK! Magazine/N&S Syndication and Licensing

Introduction

What is free speech? Why does free speech matter? Those are the questions to which my discussion will be addressed. They have been answered in different ways by different political thinkers and, even if there were no more to it than that, the fact would be enough to recommend my subject to anyone who takes an interest in ideas. But there is much more to it, for these are questions of pressing practical concern. That is one point upon which I'm pretty sure that you, the reader, will agree with me. Why else would you have chosen to open this book?

Of course, this is by no means the first or the only book about free speech ever to have been written. There are plenty of others. Even so, I should like to think that, with this one, I am making a necessary contribution to the literature. That is because the subject comes so heavily laden with emotional baggage. It is no accident that arguments surrounding it tend to be freighted with polemic, exaggeration and half-truth. At least, that is true of debates conducted in the more accessible regions of the public sphere – in the press and the broadcasting media for example. Philosophical accounts of free speech have been more careful but, as I write, they have tended to remain unappreciated. That is no accident either. These days, the arguments contained in textbooks of philosophy are sometimes expressed in terms so technical that they can intimidate the general reader.

It is with such considerations in mind that I have tried to take a step back and cast a cool eye over the intellectual terrain. I have also tried to describe that terrain in terms which are as clear and as straightforward as I can make them. As for structure, the book is divided into four chapters of roughly equal length. In the first, I describe the problems any defence of free speech must endeavour to solve and the objectives it must strive to meet. In the second I consider the connection between free speech and the pursuit of truth and, in the third, the relation between free speech and democracy. If I am not mistaken, those are the connections with which those who care about free speech tend to be most concerned. People also tend to insist upon a connection between free speech and personal autonomy or, to put it another way, upon their right to be treated as grown-ups, and not as infants whose ears need to be protected from unpalatable or offensive expressions of opinion. It's an idea to which we shall be returning at various points throughout this discussion. In the fourth chapter, I consider the relationship between arguments for free speech and the conditions – social, economic, and technological – which have tended to prevail at different times throughout history. My assumption here is that any credible argument in defence of free speech must contain some recognition of those conditions – implicit or explicit.

To explain: The origins of liberal political thought – with its emphasis on toleration and the liberty of action and expression – can be traced to the later years of the European Reformation. Prior to that, few would have questioned the morality of persecuting individuals for holding the 'wrong' opinions. Even Saint Augustine was happy with the idea that heretics should be tortured, if only for their own good. Writing in or around 400AD, he described such torture as a matter of being cruel to be kind; 'a work of mercy to which we ought to apply ourselves, in order that men may attain eternal life and escape eternal punishment'. In fact, Augustine had a point. Put it this way: Suppose that someone is about to cross the road, having failed to notice the enormous truck into whose path he or she is about to step. In that case, you would be justified in pushing that person out of harm's way – i.e. in using a certain amount of necessary force. So much seems obvious. Shouldn't it be equally obvious, then, that you should use any force necessary to persuade people for whom you care to renounce the doctrines to which they subscribe if you believe – *really* believe – that they will go to hell unless they do? Suffering in hell forever is probably even worse than being hit by a truck, so it is arguable that you should.

By the early years of the seventeenth century, however, the position exemplified by Augustine's argument had lost any appeal it may once have possessed. Why should that have been? The answer is that, between the earlier period and the later, centuries of violent religious conflict had intervened – the Reformation in other words. It was a conflict which resulted in stalemate and, consequently, in a recognition of the necessity for toleration between the adherents of different religions. As a result, the earliest defences of free speech are specifically concerned with religious toleration. To take just one, albeit famous example, John Milton's *Areopagitica*, published in 1644 is the essay in which Milton pours scorn upon a proposal by Oliver Cromwell's Puritan government to impose a system of religious censorship; a system resembling that employed by Catholic authorities in mainland Europe. '[A]s good almost kill a Man as kill a good Booke', Milton writes, 'who kills a Man kills a reasonable creature, God's image; but hee who destroyes a good Booke, kills reason iteselfe'. 1644 is not so long ago – not when you consider that the history of western thought stretches back for over two millennia. Even so, we should assume that, just as considerable changes took place between Augustine's time and Milton's, so things have changed a great deal between Milton's time and now – and in ways relevant to the present discussion.

As I have already indicated, this is primarily a work of philosophy. I make no apology for that, and it is, perhaps, symptomatic of the present intellectual climate that I should even feel that I might have to. It is the business of philosophy to deal with arguments; to analyse existing arguments and to construct new ones in the hope that they will be an improvement upon the former. These are necessary activities. Accordingly, it has been my aim throughout to set out the main arguments surrounding free speech as clearly and as systematically as I can. It is essential to have a grasp of them – the assumptions on which they are based, the way they hang together, their strengths and weaknesses – if we are to gain a clear appreciation of what is really at issue here.

Questions of
definition

My aim in this chapter is to describe the problems any credible attempt at a defence of free speech must aim to solve. It is, as I said, a 'survey of the terrain'.

Let me begin with a few statements of the obvious. I shall take it that ...

1 To exercise the right to free speech is perform an act of a certain type.

2 There is a *moral right* to free speech if people ought – morally ought – to be free to perform acts of that type.

3 There is a *legal right* to free speech if certain acts are afforded special legal protection on the grounds that they instantiate the exercise of the right to free speech.

4 In the ideal situation, legal principle will reflect moral principle. In other words, the acts people morally ought to be free to perform (statement 2) will be protected by the relevant law (statement 3).

If those assumptions strike you as so obviously true that they are hardly worth stating, so much the better. Any argument which aspires to be taken seriously is helped if it can start out from premises which it would be wilfully perverse to deny. Unfortunately though, these statements don't get us very far. One reason is this: There are many acts – acts involving speech – which it would be hard to count as instantiating the exercise of free speech, at least, there is no seriously credible interpretation of that right from which it would follow that they count as such.

Consider:

▶ You lock yourself in a room, make sure that no-one can hear you, and proceed to read extracts from your favourite text out loud.

▶ You take a spray can and decorate walls with inane slogans – 'I LIKE GIRLS' and 'KERMIT LOVES MISS PIGGY'.

In the former case, while you may be described as exercising the right to do as you please in the privacy of your own home, it would be wrong to say that, in so doing, you are also exercising the right which people normally have in mind when discussing free speech. For one thing, because you speak to no-one, and because nobody can hear you, your action lacks the *publicity* by which the genuine exercise of free speech is characterized. In the second case, your action appears too pointless and trivial to merit special protection.

▶ What free speech is not

With all that in mind, let us now turn to the following question: For what reasons might an act involving speech nevertheless fail to qualify for legal protection on the grounds that it is an exercise of the moral right to freedom of speech?

In recent times, answers to it have tended to focus upon *offensiveness* with some arguing that the right to free speech should be limited when it becomes offensive to this or that group, and others that, for example, 'there is no right not to be offended'. Controversies over offensiveness can become emotionally charged however – so much so that it can be difficult to appraise them impartially. If we are to gain a clear picture, it would be better to start elsewhere. Accordingly, I will begin with the *triviality* by which so much published material is characterized. I will then turn to *pointlessness*, and move on to offensiveness only after that.

Triviality

The following passage is drawn from the pages of *OK*, a magazine which describes itself as 'no.1 for celebrity news'.

> *CINDY'S STYLISH PIZZA CHEF: Supermodel Cindy Crawford has revealed what really happened the day Harry Styles popped round to her house to make pizza for dinner. The 47-year-old star is surely the coolest mum on the block after the One Direction singer, 19, showed up at her Malibu pad to give tips to son Presley, 14, and daughter Kaia, 11.*

The passage typifies a certain style of 'celebrity gossip' journalism, and I have selected it, only for its representative character. *OK* regularly carries several equally trivial stories, as does its rival publication, *Hello* magazine, and as do most 'red-top' tabloids in a typical week. So, can it be argued that there is a moral right to free speech such that *OK*'s freedom to publish this type of material should be legally protected? I think it would be hard to do so. The story is so trivial.

Points to note here are these: First, I am not suggesting that *OK* should be censored or suppressed. Its triviality may render it ineligible for special protection but, by the same token, neither is there any good reason for banning it. Second, I am taking it that, where there is a *right* to perform actions of a certain type, there are reasons for protecting the freedom to do those actions, even when there are good, 'countervailing' reasons for suppressing that freedom. That is part of *what it means* to say that there is a right. As the point is sometimes put, it is a feature of rights that they 'trump' those other considerations. The point will be familiar to anyone acquainted with contemporary political philosophy. It is more than 'merely academic' however, for appeals to 'national security', 'economic efficiency' and similar invocations of the public good are just the reasons to which governments do tend to appeal when seeking to suppress dissent. Considered in isolation, these may be perfectly good reasons, and not easily dismissed. We need to know what grounds there may be for protecting speech, *even when they can be persuasively invoked*.

By way of illustration, compare *OK*'s Cindy Crawford story with the reports, first carried by *The Guardian* and the *New York Times* in 2013, that the USA's National Security Agency is engaged in wholesale surveillance (aka 'The Snowden Affair'). In defence of the latter it might be argued, for example, that the citizens of a democracy have a moral right to be kept informed of their government's activities. No such considerations exist in the case of the Crawford story. The main reason for describing it as 'trivial' lies in the absolute ordinariness of the events it narrates. It must happen every day that hundreds of thousands of women invite some local teenager to have tea with their own teenage children and, if these events go unreported, that must certainly be thanks to the fact that no one except the parties directly involved is likely to take the slightest interest in them. The *OK* story is only notable for the fact that it concerns 'celebrities' – a supermodel and a member of a popular boy-band. Otherwise it would be of no consequence at all.

Well-known platitudes are lurking here, so let me put it this way: Suppose that, for whatever reason, Cindy Crawford were to object to *OK*'s having published the story about her tea-time invitation to Harry Styles. (I have no idea what that reason might be, but that's irrelevant.) Suppose that she were to go so far as to take *OK* to court. Now suppose that *OK* were to enlist Voltaire in its defence. (I don't mean the real Voltaire. I mean the apocryphal Voltaire – the Voltaire who is alleged to have said, 'I disagree with what you say, but I will defend to the death your right to say it'.) Imagine Voltaire standing up in court and saying, 'I disagree with *OK*'s statement that Harry Styles popped round to Cindy Crawford's house to make pizza, etcetera, but I will defend to the death ... etcetera.' (*To the death*, mind.) You only have to picture this *Monty Python*esque scenario to appreciate its absurdity. There being nothing more to the story, there would in fact be no good reason for dismissing Ms. Crawford's objection to the invasion of her privacy. Moreover, and though it might appear so at first glance, nor is my story as frivolous as all that, for – in fact – the popular press frequently does commit invasions of privacy, against the wishes of its victims, merely in order to satisfy a public taste for tittle-tattle. The example raises the question of how, in the absence of a plausible 'free speech' justification, it can possibly defend such activities.

I disagree with what you say ....etc.: The famous line was first attributed to Voltaire in a biography, *The Friends of Voltaire*, written by Evelyn Beatrice Hall (aka S.G.Tallentyre) and published in 1906. There is no evidence that Voltaire himself ever said any such thing.

Again – to take another popular truism – given that *OK*'s story is, no doubt, true, and supposing that there are top-flight politicians, captains of industry, judges, generals and the like who sometimes pass their time leafing through the pages of *OK* – and for all we know there may well be – then it will be equally true that *OK* 'speaks truth to power'. It is sometimes said to be the duty of the press to do just that – but in this case, so what? It's impossible to believe that a knowledge of Ms Crawford's invitation to Mr Styles could possibly affect the policies initiated by such individuals, either for good or ill. It follows, again, that it would be disingenuous if *OK* were to invoke a 'right to free speech' in support of its publication of the Cindy Crawford story.

Finally before moving on, I should recognize that my argument is potentially open to a 'slippery slope' objection. It's an objection which, I am sure, some readers will be wanting to raise and it states that, while *OK*-style celebrity gossip may be trivial, it forms a small part of something larger and more significant. Perhaps they will urge that a free press is a bastion of a free and democratic society, and that any attempt to silence the press – even an attempt to suppress a minor item of celebrity gossip – threatens to undermine the institution as a whole. In short, they may want to invoke a 'slippery slope' argument.

But such arguments are rarely persuasive. Consider the following.

Argument One:

1 I have now eaten my sandwich. I think I'll throw the wrapper into the street.

2 But, if I were to do that, others might follow my example – it would be the beginning of a slippery slope – and if everyone in the vicinity were to throw their waste paper into the street, the street would be covered in litter. Everything would be a complete mess.

Therefore,

3 I had better not throw the wrapper into the street.

Argument Two:

1 I should like to drive from London to Brighton this morning.

2 But, if I were to do that, others might follow my example – it would be the beginning of a slippery slope – and if the entire population of London (about eight million) were to choose, just now, to drive to Brighton, there would be a massive traffic jam, terrible pollution and nobody would get anywhere.

Therefore,

3 I had better not drive to Brighton.

Argument Three:

1 (Said by a judge): I should like to uphold Ms Crawford's claim against *OK* magazine.

2 But, if I were to do that it would be the beginning of a slippery slope, the freedom of the press would be so threatened that our free and democratic society would be in serious jeopardy.

Therefore,

3 I had better not allow Ms Crawford's claim against *OK*.

It should be clear that, in each of the above cases, the credibility of the argument hinges upon the likelihood that the state of affairs envisaged at step two will actually transpire. It is, thus, only too well-known that, where one person litters carelessly, others are encouraged to follow suit, which means that Argument One supplies quite a good reason for not throwing one's sandwich-wrapper into the street. By contrast, it is vanishingly improbable that the entire population of London will decide to drive to Brighton at just the same moment. It follows that Argument Two is thoroughly unpersuasive. Likewise, in the case of Argument Three – which is the objection at issue – to find it persuasive you would have to believe that nearly everyone who has ever featured as the subject of a piece in *OK* is likely to object and, further that, were this to happen, the fabric of our free, open and democratic society would be seriously threatened. None of this is at all likely or credible.

ASSERT YOUR RIGHTS!

Article 6, Section 2, of the Constitution of the United States says: "This Constitution shall be the *supreme law of the Land*."

Article 1 (Amendment) says: "Congress shall make no law respecting an establishment of religion, or *prohibiting the free exercise thereof*."

Article 9 (Amendment) says: "The enumeration in the Constitution of certain rights, shall not be construed to deny or disparge others retained by the people."

The Socialist Party says that any individual or officers of the law entrusted with the administration of conscription regulations, violate the provisions of the United States Constitution, the Supreme Law of the Land, when they refuse to recognize your right to assert your opposition to the draft.

If you are conscientiously opposed to war, if you believe in the commandment "thou shalt not kill," then that is your religion, and you shall not be prohibited from the free exercise thereof.

In exempting clergymen and members of the Society of Friends (popularly called Quakers) from active military service, the examination boards have discriminated against you.

If you do not assert and support your rights, you are helping to "deny or disparage rights" which it is the solemn duty of all citizens and residents of the United States to retain.

Here in this city of Philadelphia was signed the immortal Declaration of Independence. As a citizen of "the cradle of American Liberty" you are doubly charged with the duty of upholding the rights of the people.

Will you let cunning politicians and a mercenary capitalist press wrongly and untruthfully mould your thoughts? Do not forget your right to elect officials who are opposed to conscription.

In lending tacit or silent consent to the conscription law, in neglecting to assert your rights, you are (whether unknowingly or not) helping to condone and support a most infamous and insidious conspiracy to abridge and destroy the sacred and cherished rights of a free people. You are a citizen, not a subject! You delegate your power to the officers of the law to be used for your good and welfare, not against you.

They are your servants. Not your masters. Their wages come from the expenses of government which you pay. Will you allow them to unjustly rule you? The fathers who fought and bled to establish a free and independent nation here in America were so opposed to the militarism of the old world from which they had escaped; so keenly alive to the dangers and hardships they had undergone in fleeing from political, religious and military oppression, that they handed down to us "certain rights which must be retained by the people.

They held the spirit of militarism in such abhorrence and hate, they were so apprehensive of the formation of a military machine that would insidiously and secretly advocate the invasion of other lands, that they limited the power of Congress over the militia in providing only for the calling forth of "the militia to execute laws of the Union, suppress insurrections and repel invasions." (See general powers' of Congress, Article 1, Section 8, Paragraph 15.)

No power was delegated to send our citizens away to foreign shores to shoot up the people of other lands, no matter what may be their internal or international disputes.

The people of this country did not vote in favor of war. At the last election they voted against war. To draw this country into the horrors of the present war in Europe, to force the youth of our land into the shambles and bloody trenches of war-crazy nations, would be a crime the magnitude of which defies description. Words could not express the condemnation such cold-blooded ruthlessness deserves.

Will you stand idly by and see the Moloch of Militarism reach forth across the sea and fasten its tentacles upon this continent? Are you willing to submit to the degradation of having the Constitution of the United States treated as a "mere scrap of paper?"

Do you know that patriotism means a love for your country and not hate for others?

Will you be led astray by a propaganda of jingoism masquerading under the guise of patriotism?

No specious or plausible pleas about a "war for democracy" can becloud the issue. Democracy can not be shot into a nation. It must come spontaneously and purely from within.

Democracy must come through liberal education. Upholders of military ideas are unfit teachers. To advocate the persecution of other peoples through the prosecution of war is an insult to every good and wholesome American tradition.

"These are the times that try men's souls."

"Eternal vigilance is the price of liberty."

You are responsible. You must do your share to maintain, support and uphold the rights of the people of this country.

In this world crisis where do you stand? Are you with the forces of liberty and light or war and darkness?

(OVER)

▲ 'Schenk's pamphlet'

Pointlessness

In the course of a well-known judgment, the American Supreme Court judge, Justice Oliver Wendell Holmes, said this.

> *The most stringent protection of free speech would not protect a man in falsely shouting fire in a theatre and causing a panic.*

Actually, Wendell Holmes's judgment is well known, mainly for having been cited so often by philosophers and legal theorists in their discussions of free speech. That's why we shall also have to consider any lessons it may turn out to contain.

Notice, then, that Wendell Holmes's remark is open to two different interpretations. On the one hand, you could take him to be asserting that the restriction of free speech may be justified in times of danger and national emergency. On this point, it's relevant to note that he was speaking in 1919, not long after the end of World War One, and that he was delivering judgment in the case of *Schenck versus United States*. Schenck was in court for having organized the printing of pamphlets urging resistance to conscription into the military and their circulation to young men who were eligible for it, thereby contravening the Espionage Act of 1917. This interpretation is supported by Wendell Holmes's subsequent comments that, 'The question in every case is whether the words used are used in such circumstances and are of such a nature as to create a clear and present danger that they will bring about the substantive evils that Congress has a right to prevent' and that, 'When a nation is at war, many things that might be said in time of peace are such a hindrance to its effort that their utterance will not be endured so long as men fight'. On this interpretation, Schenk's action is analogous to shouting fire in a theatre (according to Holmes) in the sense that both are likely to cause an evil which ought to be prevented (panic and mayhem in the former case, subversion of the government's military strategy in the latter).

Now, if you familiarise yourself with the case, you may or may not come to the conclusion that the court was right in judging Schenk's actions to have been seditious. But that is not the point here. Rather, the point is that, when interpreted in this way, Wendell Holmes is arguing that the right must be limited, even to the extent that it cannot cover the freedom to criticize the military policy of one's own government. If you think a right to free speech should include the right to do just that, then you will find Wendell Holmes's position unacceptable.

But there is an alternative interpretation of his remark. Put it this way: Imagine a person – call this person, P – who gets his kicks in the following way: Every Saturday evening, P goes to the theatre or, as may be, the cinema. Having chosen a seat, and settled into it, P waits until the performance is well under way, at which point P leaps to his feet and screams, 'Fire!' P resumes his seat and enjoys watching the panic and mayhem which ensue. Now suppose that P is arrested, taken to court, and that in his defence P pleads that he was merely exercising his right to free speech. Such a claim would surely be absurd, and if *that* is Wendell Holmes's point we have to agree with him. (It's an interpretation which is supported by his reference to someone who *falsely* shouts fire. In my story, the whole point so far as P is concerned is the fun he gets.) So far as I can see, there could be absolutely no point in protecting a person's 'right' to cause panic and mayhem, simply for his or her own enjoyment, and quite a lot to be said against the protection of any such 'right'. The example illustrates a general point, then, namely that any persuasive definition of free speech must draw a convincing line between those actions whose protection would be, as it were, *pointless*, and those which ought to be protected.

The 'controversialist', the late Christopher Hitchens, was apt to begin his lectures on free speech by shouting 'Fire! Fire!' Looking dramatically around, Hitchens would then announce, e.g. 'Now you've heard it!' Unsurprisingly, the audience would remain seated in respectful silence. The performance was completely beside the point. If Hitchens had really wanted to test Wendell Holmes's judgment he would have made it, incognito, to the nearest cinema and waited until the film was halfway through before shouting 'Fire!', and he would then have been able to test the audience's reaction.

Offensiveness

With that, let us now turn to the question of offensiveness, and to the following claim.

There is no such thing as the right not to be offended.

Is this true? I'm asking, partly because quite a number of formidable individuals – including some distinguished intellectuals – subscribe to the claim. I find this surprising because, so far as I can see, it is not just false, but obviously so. At least, it is if you take it at face value. Consider: Suppose that some person is in the habit of singling out passers-by at random and abusing them verbally. As before, we may as well call this person, P. As the passers-by approach, each in turn, they are confronted by P, who shouts, for example, 'Oy you! Uglymug! You smell!' (Substitute your favourite terms of abuse here.) Such behaviour would be offensive, would it not? Now ask; does P have a right to engage in such behaviour? By that, I mean does P have a moral right, one which ought to be recognized in, and enforced by law? So far as I can see, the answer can only be that P has no such right. On the contrary, it seems to me that people have a moral right to go about their daily business without falling prey to such abusive behaviour. This being the case, it follows directly that there ought to be a corresponding legal right (although the point hardly needs labouring, given that the right is already recognized in all civilized societies in the form of various prohibitions against abusive behaviour, harassment, and the like).

But if it is so evident that there that there is such a thing as the right not to be offended, how can it be that so many intellectually sophisticated people can insist, and so forcefully, that no such right exists? How can the late Ronald Dworkin, Quain Professor of Jurisprudence at University College London have insisted that 'in a democracy no one, however powerful or important, can have a right not to be insulted or offended', and Sir Salman Rushdie, the distinguished author, that, 'There is no right in the world not to be offended. That right simply doesn't exist'. And those are just two examples. Try typing 'no right not to be offended' into Google, and you will come up with a great many more. (My own random and rather cursory trawl yielded similar remarks by Shami Chakrabarti, director of the civil rights advocacy organization, 'Liberty'; Peter Tatchell, the prominent political activist; Nicholas Hytner, until recently director of the British National Theatre, Phillip Pullman, writer and – until recently – Children's Laureate, David Davies MP, Christopher Hitchens, Richard Dawkins, Stephen Fry, and the comedians John Cleese, Rowan Atkinson and Ricky Gervais.)

Offensiveness: a constructive suggestion

It would be too easy to assume that such individuals are merely blind to the obvious – so what is going on here? There is, of course, the consideration that the concepts of offensiveness and offendedness may be too inexact to capture the diverse range of actions and reactions which are, in fact, at issue. A fastidious diner may take 'offence' at a guest's slobbish table manners. The victim of racist abuse will also suffer 'offence'. But bad manners and overt racism are by no means morally equivalent, and we should not let ourselves be fooled by the fact that the same term applies in both cases into thinking that they are. But, leaving that point to one side, there is the further point that the truth is rather more nuanced than my argument up to this point has suggested and, for all I have said so far, it only follows that there is a right not to be offended, *other things being equal*. In the case of abusive P, there is, thus, no redeeming feature which might excuse or justify P's behaviour. Other things are not always equal, however, and *there may be contexts* in which the right not to be offended cannot be insisted upon.

So, here is my constructive suggestion. (Well, it's intended to be constructive at any rate.) Imagine a discussion group. Suppose that the group has been convened in order to assess certain religious doctrines for their coherence and veracity. Items to be discussed include the credibility of belief in the existence of God, various accounts of the origins of the universe, and the possibility of life after death. Suppose also that some members of the group are religious fundamentalists of one stripe or another. They believe in the literal truth of the Koran, or that Darwinian accounts of evolution, being inconsistent with the teachings of the Bible, cannot be true. Suppose that others are atheists, some of them 'militant'. It is pretty clear that, in this situation, the views of some members will be offensive to other members. Those on one side will want to cry 'blasphemy!', to which others would want to respond with 'bigotry!' and 'irrationality!', and, to the extent that being offended is a subjective matter, there would be nothing much to be done about that. (In fact, those on one side might be offended by the *mere thought* that the others held the views they do, whether or not the latter were permitted to express their views.) It is equally clear, however, that, given the situation, neither side has the right to use its own offendedness as a reason for shutting down the other's contribution to the debate. The reason should be clear: If it were to do that, the whole exercise would lose its point. This example is, thus, one illustration of *a context* within which the right not to be offended cannot be legitimately claimed and – by the same token – it describes a context within which the corresponding right to be offensive to those with whom one disagrees has to be upheld.

Now, I don't know what the individuals to whom I have been referring would make of my argument here, but I'm inclined to think that, in fact, most of them would tend to agree with me. That's because, if you consider what they say, you will see that – far from insisting upon an absolute right to be as offensive as one likes in all circumstances – each assumes a context within which it would be perverse or counterproductive to insist upon a (supposed) right not to be offended. It is, thus, Dworkin's claim that, '*in a democracy* no one, however powerful or important can have a right not to be insulted or offended'. Likewise, Salman Rushdie enlarges upon his statement that, 'There is no right in the world not to be offended' with the explanation that, '*In a free society, an open society*, people have strong opinions, and these opinions very often clash' and that, '*In a democracy*, we have to learn to deal with this'. 'This is true about novels' he says, 'it's true about cartoons, it's true about all these products'. Note that, in fact, both Dworkin and Rushdie place the claim at issue within the context of democracy. With his reference to novels and cartoons, Rushdie also places it within the context of a literary culture, broadly conceived. Likewise – to take just one more example – Rowan Atkinson's insistence that 'the right to offend is far more important than any right not to be offended,' is connected with his concern to protect an arena within which ideas can be exchanged and criticized. '[A] law which attempts to say you can criticize or ridicule ideas as long as they are not religious ideas is,' he says, ' a very peculiar law indeed'. None of these is precisely equivalent to my 'discussion group' example, but that doesn't matter. The point is that there are relevant similarities and, as I shall argue shortly, nor does it matter that the example is rather artificial.

With that, I should have said enough to illustrate the point that not every speech act can be counted a genuine exercise of free speech, although I should note – finally – that the categories I have described are by no means mutually exclusive. Abusive P's insults are thus (i) trivial in content, (ii) pointless, and (iii) a case of 'causing someone to feel deeply hurt, upset, or angry', which is how the *Oxford English Dictionary* defines 'offensive'. Why should I expect you to agree with my arguments up to this point? After all, I am not describing 'facts' which are somehow 'out there' in the world, as if I were a scientist describing some natural phenomenon. Nor am I willing to resort to that philosophers' cop-out, the 'appeal to intuition'. The best I can do is appeal to your moral sense. It is – of course – possible to imagine a society in which the freedoms to spread false alarms, and to vilify individuals at random, were defined in law as 'rights' and protected as such. I can only invite you to consider what, if anything, would be gained if that were so.

▶ Theory, practice and the 'discussion group model'

As I emphasized in my introduction. I do not share the stereotypical view that philosophy is an ivory-tower pursuit with no practical relevance. With that in mind, this would be an appropriate point at which to include a few words on the relevance of philosophy to practice. If nothing else, it will help me deal with two particular objections which – as I am sure – some readers will be wanting to raise. According to the first, I am guilty of *revisionism*. According to the second, I am being overly *pedantic*. Let me take each in turn.

First, the charge of revisionism: I have opened myself to this with my argument that the right to be offensive is context-dependent. My guess is that some readers will be inclined to see this as a kind of retreat, and think that I am in danger of defining 'free speech' in too narrow a way; perhaps in a way which fails to do justice to the rough-and-tumble character of free speech as it is actually exercised in the world at large. In reply to this – and leaving arguments I have already set out to one side – I would emphasize (i) that a recognition of the context-dependent character of the right to offend actually put us in a better position to appreciate the serious issues which are in contention here, and that it is better to deal with the real issues than to sound off in a display of impotent portentousness. In addition I would argue (ii) that, while there may be something artificial about the discussion group model as I have presented it – something a little 'academic' perhaps – it reflects an ideal which has run like a thread through arguments for free speech from the seventeenth century onwards; an ideal which is fundamental to the world-view most readers of this book will have inherited. (It is, if you like, an schematic representation of the liberal *weltanschauung*.) Both are points to which we shall be returning, repeatedly, at various junctures throughout this book's discussion.

Second, the charge of pedantry: Consider the trajectory followed by my discussion of the 'no right not to be offended' claim. I began by challenging it, but I then conceded that, when contextualised, it can be sometimes be credible. I then added that those with whom I had initially appeared to disagree also contextualise the claim. In other words, I started out by disagreeing with Dworkin, Rushdie, *et. al.* and then, after several paragraphs of argument, I ended up by *more or less* agreeing with them. Some readers will be wondering what the point of such manoeuvres can have been when – as they will think – I could have just agreed with the others in the first place and left it at that. My answer here is, again, that after the manoeuvres we should have a clearer picture of what is really at issue.

The discussion group model

By way of illustration, consider the model more closely and, as a start, note the following.

1 It places 'offensiveness' in a certain perspective. Thus, each participant in the discussion must certainly be

free to express views *whose content* may be offensive to other participants (the religious to express views which others think irrational, atheists to express irreligious views, and so on). Such views would, of course, include views that the opinions of others are stupid, ignorant, immoral, nasty, *etcetera*. Unless this were the case, it would be impossible for the discussion to proceed. (So – note – I am not suggesting that the exercise of free speech should be decorous or restrained. Like J.S.Mill, I disagree with 'those who say, that the free expression of all opinions should be permitted, on condition that the manner be temperate, and do not pass the bounds of fair discussion.) Even so, other forms of offensive behaviour *are* ruled out by the model, although they are disqualified, not so much by their offensiveness, as by their potential to prevent the discussion from continuing. Heckling is thereby ruled out, but only when it has crossed a certain threshold of disruptiveness. Preventing others from expressing their views by shouting them down is certainly ruled out, as is intimidating them to the extent that they are afraid to speak.

2 In the group, each participant confronts the others on equal terms, in this case – because the group is a discussion group – that means treating the opinions of others as equally deserving of rational consideration. You could say that there is a certain etiquette involved, each participant being constrained to consider the opinions of the others, even though each may think the others' views completely stupid or insane. In short, it's complicated, and it doesn't help to focus upon offensiveness to the exclusion of other factors.

3 In the group, no individual can be assumed to have full possession of the truth, or to have special authority to determine the outcome of the discussion. If that were to happen the point of the exercise would be lost or, as it may be, perverted.

Now consider the similarities between this model and the contexts assumed by the individuals I discussed earlier. Thus, in a democracy (Dworkin) people confront each other as equal participants in the decision-making process, and especially as voters. No-one can be assumed to have special authority to determine the outcome of the process. Likewise, the novel (according to Rushdie) 'does not seek to establish a privileged language, but it insists on the freedom to portray and analyse the struggle between the different contestants for such privileges', and literature is 'the one place in any society where, within the secrecy of our own heads, we can hear voices talking about everything in every possible way.' An arena within which ideas and attitudes are freely pitted against each other (Atkinson) is – well – an arena within which ideas and attitudes are pitted against each other.

So, the practical relevance of the discussion group model, lies in the way it supplies a measuring device. I mean that the greater the resemblance between the model and some situation about which we may be trying to form a judgement, the more the categories applicable to the former apply to the latter. We may ask – for example – are we dealing with a 'speech act' which can be regarded as, in some way, a contribution to the democratic decision-making process here, or to our literary culture, or (in the case of such-and-such a cartoon or joke) with an exercise of the freedom to criticize ideas? If we are, then the offensiveness of the act cannot be a reason for censoring it – not if we value democracy, or literature, or intellectual exchange.

On the other hand, there are cases which bear far less resemblance to the discussion group example than they do to that of randomly abusive P. These include instances of what has come to be known as 'hate speech'. For an illustration, imagine, 'A man out walking with his seven-year-old son and his ten-year-old daughter'. '[He] turns a corner on a city street in new Jersey and is confronted with a sign [which] says: "Muslims and 9/11! Don't serve them, don't speak to them, and don't let them in'. Suppose the daughter asks, "What does it mean papa?" I am borrowing the example from a recent book by Jeremy Waldron. Waldron continues the narrative by picturing the father hurrying the children on, hoping they will not come across any more of the signs.

As Waldron (rightly) observes, these signs convey messages. To the Muslim community they say, 'Don't be fooled into thinking you are welcome here. The society around you may seem to be hospitable and nondiscriminatory; but the truth is that you are not wanted, and you and your families will be shunned, excluded, beaten, and driven out.' To the community at large, they say, 'We know some of you agree that these people are not wanted here. We know that some of you feel that they are dirty (or dangerous or criminal or terrorist). Know now that you are not alone. Whatever the government says, there are enough of us around to make sure these people are not welcome. 'That's the point of these signs,' says Waldron, 'that's the point of hate speech – to send these messages'.

To put it in my terms, such messages resemble threats more than they do contributions to a discussion, and there is no reason to suppose that the liberty to issue them is defensible in terms appropriate to the latter. In my opinion, this is a useful result. That's because I think that, at present, many people are genuinely exercised by (what they see as) the tension between the right to free speech and the need to respect the sensitivities of vulnerable groups. More often than not, its resolution is said to require a straight 'trade-off' between the two. As Dworkin puts it in the piece from which I quoted earlier, there is a 'widely held opinion that freedom of speech has limits [and] that it must be balanced against the virtues of "multiculturalism"'. But that way of representing the tension underplays differences between the contexts within which words may be uttered (or written), or so I am suggesting, and thereby obscures a possible solution to a genuine difficulty.

▶ 'Free speech' or 'freedom of expression'?

In 1972, the American philosopher, T.M.Scanlon, published an influential article entitled 'A Theory of Freedom of Expression'. In it, Scanlon describes the task of 'a doctrine of freedom of expression' as being to 'single out a class of "protected acts" which it holds to be immune from restrictions to which other acts are subject'. He defines an 'act of expression' as 'any act that is intended by its agent to communicate to one or more persons some proposition or attitude', and adds that the class of such acts is extremely broad, 'In addition to many acts of speech and publication', he says, 'it includes displays of symbols, failures to display them, demonstrations, many musical performances, and some bombings, assassinations, and self-immolations'. The liberty Scanlon calls 'freedom of expression' is, of course, more or less equivalent to what I am calling 'freedom of speech'. Also, it should be clear from the lines quoted that I am in broad agreement with Scanlon's conception of the task facing any theorist attempting to frame a defence of that freedom. Even so, here, it's worth my adding a couple of comments on Scanlon's way of putting things.

The first relates to the most obvious difference between Scanlon and myself, namely his use of the term 'freedom of expression' for what I have been calling 'free speech'. In fact, Scanlon's usage is now the norm, and writers on this subject routinely refer to 'freedom of speech and expression' or simply to 'freedom of expression'. Even so, I propose to deviate from normal practice and stick with 'free speech'. Let me first explain why, and then explain why this is not a quibble.

Consider, then, two paintings by the same artist. Let's take Picasso's *Guernica* and one of his portraits – let's say his *Seated Nude* of 1909–10. As many readers will know, *Guernica*, with its images of panic, pain and violent destruction – its rearing horse, dismembered bodies, its mother screaming in terror – embodies Picasso's horrified reaction to the aerial bombardment of Guernica, the Basque town, in 1937. It was an atrocity perpetrated by German forces, acting on behalf of General Franco, during the Spanish Civil War. In other words, Picasso was *making a statement* with his painting, even though the production of *Guernica* did not involve the use of speech – so that it was not a 'speech act' in the literal sense – and even though Picasso evidently felt that mere words wouldn't be up to the job it took his images to do. ('It isn't up to the painter to define the symbols,' he said, 'Otherwise it would be better if he wrote them out in so many words!') It was, as Scanlon puts it, a matter of 'communicating some proposition or attitude'. Moreover, the fact that, later in 1937, it was exhibited in the Spanish pavilion of the Paris exhibition means that it was a public act. Picasso didn't march around with a placard bearing the slogan 'Down With Franco!' (How comparatively ineffectual that would have been!) Even so – and although it may be an understated way of putting the point – it would be true to say that he was expressing an attitude and a point of view, and placing it 'out there' in the public arena.

It is for such reasons that I would describe the production and exhibiting of *Guernica* as an exercise of free speech, even though it was not – or not literally – an act of speaking. (So here we have a further difficulty which any credible account of free speech must confront. We have already noted that many acts involving speech do

▲ *Guernica* by Picasso.

not qualify as instantiating the exercise of free speech. It now transpires that certain acts involving rather more than speech – and some which involve no speech at all – do so qualify.) By contrast, *Seated Nude*, while it may exemplify a revolutionary development in the history of art, while its use of colour and its treatment of the image may be original and striking, and while it may have provoked heated controversy, cannot be described as the positioning of a statement and/or an attitude within the public forum, or, at least, not without triviality. (I say 'not without triviality, because it could – of course – be said to advance propositions such as, 'Look! here is a different way to paint a seated nude!') *Seated Nude* is an early exercise in 'analytical cubism'. With it, Picasso seeks to, as it were, analyse the painting's somewhat conventional subject (the nude) and reconstruct it in a new way, but the painting speaks to nothing outside art itself. It is, thus, the outcome of an act of expression – in this case an act of artistic expression – but it does not reflect the exercise of free speech.

▲ *Seated Nude: Picasso, 1909-10*

For the remainder of my discussion, then, I shall reserve the expression 'free speech' for acts which may be said to advance a proposition (i.e. to 'make a statement') in public, either literally as in the case of publication or of carrying a placard, or to all intents and purposes as in that of the production and display of *Guernica*. (In certain circumstances, even wearing a t-shirt, or drinking from a mug, can count as of such.)

In 1983, during the apartheid period, a South African court sentenced a factory worker, Mathews Ntshiwa, for having a mug bearing the slogan, 'Release Nelson Mandela'. At his trial, Ntshiwa said, 'I only used to drink tea out of the mug'.

My point is that, while every exercise of free speech (in my sense) is, by its very nature, an act of expression, some acts of expression are only the latter, the production of *Seated Nude* being a case in point. In insisting upon this, I am, in fact, imposing a distinction which is a little more rigid than that reflected in ordinary, day-to-day discourse. But I shall insist upon it nevertheless, even though the two freedoms – of speech and of expression – are closely related, and even though there are familiar cases which give rise to issues relating to both. Just for example, some reasons for defending freedom of speech, however offensive it might be, may be paralleled in arguments for the freedom to exhibit certain works of art, however offensive or pornographic they may be thought by some. On the other hand though, in the case of artistic expression it may turn out that there are culturally determined norms – norms of taste and tastelessness – which may be legitimately invoked in the cause of censorship, but which should not be used to justify the suppression of free speech. In short, it is important to keep things clear.

Free speech and technology

My remaining comments on Scanlon's conception of the task facing any 'theory of freedom of expression' relate to his assertion (quoted earlier) that the 'protected' category it sets out to define must include a wide and diverse range of acts (including displays of symbols, failures to display them, demonstrations, and so on). As I said, he is right about this, but then, it is hardly news that a credible defence of free speech must include rather more than the mere freedom to communicate by using one's voice. Any modern person would expect as much. In fact, to get back to a time when the use of the voice was the only method of communication available, you would probably have to return to the Bronze Age, when messages from beyond the village were proclaimed by heralds to its illiterate inhabitants. Arguably, the range of acts with which we ought to be concerned here began to diversify the moment writing came into existence, and it had certainly begun to do so by the time printing was invented.

It follows that, in any given time, *what counts* as an exercise of free speech must be, in part, a function of the available technology. Clearly, the publication of a book can only qualify as an instance of that exercise once printing has been invented. Otherwise there would be no book. By the same token, a new type of 'speech act', the TV broadcast, came into existence with the invention of television. Likewise, had Scanlon been writing his article now, then I guess he would have added to his list acts which have only become possible with the rise of the internet – blogging, 'tweeting' and the like. But what does this mean? Sometimes, new technology makes it possible to do *the same thing*, only more efficiently. For example, a plane will enable you to 'travel from London to New York' more rapidly than a boat could. Should we assume that, likewise, advances in communications technology supply us with improved techniques for doing the same thing, namely 'perform speech acts'?. Alternatively, could it be that, with these advances, there come changes so profound that the very character of 'what we do' is changed, so much so that the 'free speech issue' itself must be continually reconfigured? It is, at any rate, a question worth considering.

▶ From definition to value

The upshot of this chapter's discussion is that an answer to the question, 'what is free speech?' must specify a category of acts which:

1 merit special protection – 'special' in the sense that they should be protected, even when there are good 'countervailing' reasons for preventing people from doing those acts.

2 make a statement, either (i) literally – that is, with the use of the spoken or written word – or (ii) can be construed as the making of a statement. (A newspaper article stating that the bombing of Guernica was an atrocity would be an example of (i). The painting and exhibiting of *Guernica* by Picasso is an example of (ii).)

3 are public in the sense that they place an opinion or an attitude 'out there' in the public sphere.

The 'Rushdie Affair': In 1988 the then ruler of Iran, the Ayatollah Khomeini, issued a fatwa, or death threat, against the author Salman Rushdie. Rushdie's 'crime' was to have published a novel *The Satanic Verses*, in which the prophet Mohammed features as a character. Rushdie was forced to go into hiding. You can read his own account of these events in his *Joseph Anton*. As I write, the fatwa has never been officially lifted.

The 'Danish Cartoons': In 2005, the Danish newspaper, *Jyllands-Posten*, published a series of cartoons featuring the prophet Mohammed and poking fun at Islam. Various Islamic groups complained that they were blasphemous, and their publication was followed by protests, in Denmark and elsewhere. In London, demonstrators carried placards bearing slogans such as 'Exterminate those who slander Islam' and 'Freedom of Expression go to Hell'.

Charlie Hebdo: In January 2015, gunmen broke into the editorial meeting of the French satirical journal, *Charlie Hebdo*, and killed eleven people. As they escaped, they murdered another person, a policeman. Twelve others were injured, and a further five were murdered, in related attacks elsewhere in northern France. Al Qaeda claimed responsibility. *Charlie Hebdo* had also been featuring cartoons featuring the prophet Mohammed

But now, what of the further question, 'Why does free speech matter?' After all, there are plenty of acts which – being trivial, pointless, and/or merely offensive – fail to satisfy the first criterion above, even though they satisfy the second and third. In other words, for all I have said so far, the question of *precisely what* acts

▲ Paris, February 2015

merit special protection is still open, and for an answer to that we need an explanation of wherein the value of free speech lies. It is in the following chapters that we shall go in search of that explanation. That said, it only remains to note that any such explanation must operate at two levels. One is the level of the particular issue. Cases which, in one way or another, raise questions related to the value of free speech are plentiful, and readers will find it easy enough to remind themselves of some. Neo-Nazi demonstrations, 'Holocaust denial' literature, hate speech, the 'Rushdie Affair' (1988), the case of the 'Danish cartoons' (2005), the question of who should own the major newspapers and other media outlets – these are examples most likely to come to mind.

But there is also a more general level at which the question demands an answer. Here is a thought experiment: Imagine a society, the majority of whose members are reasonably happy, reasonably comfortable, and reasonably secure, but in which there is no recognition of a right to free speech. This society is run by a *junta* of well-meaning dictators. It may be totalitarian, but it is a benevolent totalitarianism. In it, most people take little interest in current affairs, national or international. (Why should they?) Nor are they especially exercised by intellectual questions. (Why should they be?) They attach no special importance to such values as 'the liberty of thought and discussion' or 'press freedom'. As for the dictators, they regard any criticism of their regime as irritatingly disruptive of the efficiency with which they institute their benevolent policies (and they are, indeed, both efficient and benevolent). It could be that such a society is no more than a theoretical possibility, but, even if it is, it presents the advocate of a liberal order with a challenge, namely to explain why the liberal way of doing things – with its respect for individual liberty and its array of protected rights – should be preferable to an efficiently working benevolent totalitarianism. That may not be so easy to do.

Free speech
and truth

▲ John Stuart Mill

If people are left free to discuss, argue and criticize each other's ideas their grasp of those ideas will usually increase – or so it is reasonable to assume. If they are to meet the criticisms of others, they will be forced to refine and restate their own arguments. They are likely to find themselves attending to fine detail – in their own arguments and those levelled against them – and they may sometimes have to pursue lines of reasoning along unlikely avenues to remote locations. Of course, it is by no means inevitable that, in every case, the exercise of the liberty to think and discuss will serve to increase the pool of knowledge and understanding available to humanity. Even so, there are good reasons for thinking that, where that liberty is guaranteed, their pursuit is more efficiently facilitated than it would be under alternative arrangements.

So much is – perhaps – plain common sense. At any rate, it is unsurprising that there should be a long-standing tradition of argument which makes a case for free speech by linking it with the pursuit of knowledge. It is a tradition whose origins can be traced right back to the origins of liberal thought in the seventeenth century. 'He that can apprehend and consider vice with all her baits and seeming pleasures, and yet abstain, and yet distinguish, and yet prefer that which is truly better, he is the true warfaring Christian', so proclaimed Milton in *Areopagitica*, his 1644 diatribe against censorship, and,

> *I cannot praise a fugitive and cloistered vertue, unexercis'd and unbreath'd, that never sallies out and sees her adversary, but slinks out of the race, where that immortall garland is to be run for, not without dust and heat. Assuredly we bring not innocence into the world, we bring impurity much rather; that which purifies us is triall, and triall is by what is contrary.*

John Milton (1608–1674): Yes, this is the very same Milton who wrote *Paradise Lost*. He was also the author of some eloquent essays. *Areopagitica* is one. It is so named after the Areopagus in Athens, a site where the council of ancient Athens met, and from where a number of famous individuals, including St Paul, delivered speeches.

These are stirring words indeed. It will be clear from the above, I think, that the knowledge which, according to Milton, can only be achieved through bracing exposure to adversarial 'triall' is moral knowledge, – knowledge of virtue and vice. But by the nineteenth century, 'the argument from truth', as I shall call it here, had become broadened and secularised. The best known version of that argument is contained in the second chapter of John Stuart Mill's famous essay, *On Liberty*. The chapter is entitled, 'Of the Liberty of Thought and Discussion'. Towards its end Mill supplies the following summary of the four 'grounds' upon which he claims to have defended the liberty of thought and discussion.

> *First, if any opinion is compelled to silence, that opinion may, for aught we can certainly know, be true. To deny this is to assume our own infallibility.*

> *Secondly, though the silenced opinion be an error, it may, and very commonly does, contain a portion of the truth; and since the general or prevailing opinion on any subject is rarely or never the whole truth, it is only by the collision of adverse opinions that the remainder of the truth has any chance of being supplied.*

> *Thirdly, even if the received opinion be not only true, but the whole truth; unless it is suffered to be, and actually is, vigorously and earnestly contested, it will, by most of those who receive it, be held in the manner of a prejudice, with little comprehension or feeling of its rational grounds. And not only this, but,*

fourthly, the meaning of the doctrine itself will be in danger of being lost or enfeebled, and deprived of its vital effect on the character and conduct; the dogma becoming a mere formal profession, inefficacious for good, but cumbering the ground and preventing the growth of any real and heartfelt conviction from reason or personal experience.

Notice how Mill draws a number of distinct connections between the freedom to think and discuss and the value of truth. The reason for which censorship is to be condemned is, thus, the manner in which it impedes the pursuit of truth (first ground). *That* is why it is tantamount to an 'assumption of infallibility' (and this applies – we may take it – even to censorship which is imposed for reasons which are, in themselves, perfectly good. Arguably, the prevention of 'offence' to others would be such a reason). It is for the sake of truth that we are enjoined to ensure that adverse opinions are free to 'collide' (second ground) and it is only where ideas are open to challenge by those opposed to them that we have a chance of fully comprehending their true import (third ground). Finally, the presence in the world of beliefs which have not been so exposed to challenge – which have degenerated to the level of 'dead dogma' – is worse than useless (fourth ground). (But – note – I'm calling this an 'argument from truth' because that is the usage favoured by Mill. However, it would be less awkward to call it an 'argument from knowledge and understanding', and, for the rest of this chapter, I shall tend to do so. That's partly because the pursuit of knowledge is, in any case, the pursuit of truth, and partly because there are certain areas – literature, history, philosophy, for example – in which one can never be sure that one has finally arrived at truth. These are, nevertheless, activities which involve the pursuit of understanding.)

Mill's *On Liberty* was published in 1859. In the same year Darwin published *On the Origin of Species by Means of Natural Selection*. These two works alone identify the year as having marked a watershed in intellectual history for, just as Darwin's account of evolution has remained by far the most influential thesis in biological science, so Mill's version of the argument from truth has remained one of the most influential arguments for free speech. Therefore, there is every reason for subjecting the argument from truth to critical examination in order to determine precisely where its strengths and weaknesses lie – and that is what I propose to do in this chapter.

John Stuart Mill (1806–1873): Mill was one of the nineteenth century's most influential political thinkers. He was brought up to be a utilitarian, like his father, James Mill and his mentor, Jeremy Bentham. Utilitarianism is the moral philosophy according to which 'the greatest good of the greatest number'. He explains and defends that philosophy in his essay, *Utilitarianism*. *On Liberty* is, by far, his most influential political work.

Stripped to its bare essentials, the argument looks like this:

A Where people are left free to argue, discuss and criticize each other's ideas, the pursuit of knowledge and understanding is – usually – facilitated.

Therefore,

B The right to free speech ought to be recognized and protected by law.

As a start, note that I shall not be especially concerned with the question of whether premise A is true. In fact, I have already suggested a few reasons for believing it to be just that. Rather, the question with which I shall be concerned in this chapter is that of whether the truth of A supports conclusion B, and here the foregoing two-sentence specification of the argument renders a potential source of difficulty perfectly apparent. It takes the form of a *non sequitur* for, whereas premise A refers to the freedom to 'argue, discuss and criticize' in the pursuit of 'knowledge and understanding', conclusion B refers to 'free speech'. There is a potential difficulty because it could turn out that the former freedom and the latter are by no means equivalent – not in all cases. The *non sequitur* reflects the way Mill's argument has been deployed since *On Liberty*'s publication. In fact, Mill himself is quite unequivocal. His argument is, just as he says, a defence of 'the liberty of thought and discussion'. 'Free speech' is an expression he never uses. Even so, it is in defence of the broader freedom, 'free speech', that others have tended to draw upon the case he makes.

Accordingly, I shall open my discussion with an account of certain problem cases, that is, cases whose problematic character derives from the fact that, while they are often held to involve the exercise of the right to free speech, it is nevertheless difficult to see how the argument from truth can be brought to bear upon them. Their problematic character also reflects certain features of the argument's general structure, so I shall then go on to consider those features. Finally, I shall turn to Mill's own view of the social changes which had taken place in the decades preceding *On Liberty*'s publication in 1859, and their relevance to the argument from truth.

▶ Problem cases

The neo-Nazi spectacular

The National Front (UK) is a fascist political party with a racist agenda. (As I write, the NF claims, on its website, to 'uphold the wish of the majority of British people for Britain to remain a white country' and advocates a policy of repatriation for non-whites.) It has a US counterpart in the National Socialist White Peoples' Party (NSWPP). The activities of the former were illustrated in an especially dramatic way by events which took place on April 23rd 1979 in Southall, a London Borough whose population is predominantly composed of first, second, and third generation immigrants, most of whom hail from the South-Asian sub-continent. On that day, the NF proposed to march to the town hall, where they had been granted the legal right to hold an election meeting. A counter-demonstration was organized, the police moved in, things got out of hand and one demonstrator, Blair

Peach, was killed. As for the NSWPP, it is noted, more often than not in textbooks of legal theory, for having planned a similar march through Skokie, a Chicago suburb with a preponderantly Jewish population, many of whom were Holocaust survivors. As things turned out, however, the march never took place.

Of course, these are events which took place some decades ago, and they suggest that – in 'the West' at least – neo-Nazis were more active in the 1970s than they are now. (In those years, the NSWPP would hold rallies in Chicago's Marquette Park, in an area then known for its febrile, racially tense, atmosphere. On at least one occasion, they marched into a nearby black neighbourhood, some wearing Nazi uniform, and some carrying signs reading 'White Power' and 'Beware Nigger'.) However, there is no reason to suppose that neo-fascism won't enjoy a resurgence, so it's worth pausing to consider the recurring pattern exemplified by the events in Southall and those which might have taken place in Skokie. Features they share are as follows.

i   Each is orchestrated by a small and somewhat cranky group. (These days, can there really be more than a few people who want to be governed by a bunch of strutting comic book Nazis, complete with uniforms and swastika armbands?)

ii   Even so, they mine prejudices (racism and xenophobia) which are widespread throughout the population.

iii There is a likelihood that they will cause their targets hurt. (After all, they are intended to intimidate.)

iv They have been thought by some to raise serious issues concerning free speech. Just for example, the authors of a report into the Southall disturbances express the hope that a way of preventing a recurrence of such events can be found, 'consistent with the maintenance of legitimate rights to free speech'. In the case of Skokie, an order restricting the marchers' activities, imposed by the county Circuit Court, was overturned by the US Supreme Court on the grounds that it violated first amendment rights. Even the swastika itself was ruled to be a symbolic form of free speech entitled to first amendment protections.

Here, the salient relationship is that between (iii) and (iv). That's because, other things being equal, the likelihood of their causing hurt would be quite sufficient to justify the prohibition of such events if it were not *also* true that free speech is at risk in these cases. In fact, it might be sufficient, even if the likelihood were small and the hurt relatively insignificant. In other words, the reasons for and against tolerating such events would be neither more nor less applicable than they would in other cases of gratuitously offensive, insulting behaviour. (As an outsider, I find it impossible to judge the degree of hurt suffered in these cases. In his account of the Skokie affair, Ariel Neir comments that, 'The resistance of Skokie's Jews to a proposed demonstration in their town by American Nazis was a kind of delayed response of anger about the past', which suggests that some were welcoming a chance to 'get' the Nazis, at last. But he also describes the 'terrible memories' suffered by the survivors. 'One man recalls seeing an SS man shove a poker hot from the fire down a young boy's throat until the boy was dead'. Others saw relatives being badly beaten up before being gassed or buried alive. Who knows what feelings such marches can arouse in those at whom they are directed?)

As I have just remarked, however, if the Nazis were genuinely exercising a right to free speech in these cases, – a moral right which ought to be legally defended – then there would be a reason, a *special* reason, for tolerating their activities. So, were they? Well, the answer is that for all I have said so far they may have been but that, if they were, the point remains to be established with the help of some argument *other than* the argument from truth. Clearly, any attempt to defend the actions of the Nazis in Southall and Skokie with *that* argument would have to portray them engaged in the pursuit of truth through the exercise of argument, or, as Mill puts it, as exercising 'liberty of thought and discussion'. But wouldn't it be fantastical to describe those who stand on the Town Hall steps and taunt the crowd with Hitler salutes, as at Southall, or, as in Chicago, march around with banners declaring 'Niggers Out!' as engaged in any such activity? Of course it would.

Holocaust denial

Proponents of (what has come to be known as) 'Holocaust denial' seek to mitigate Nazi Germany's reputation for having committed mass murder on an unprecedented scale. Holocaust deniers typically claim that:

i there never were any gas chambers, either at Auschwitz or any other camp ii the figure of six million – generally agreed to be the number of Jews murdered by the Nazis – is a gross exaggeration: In fact, there were a few hundred thousands, comparable to the number of Russians who died in the siege of Leningrad or of Germans killed in Allied air raids.

iii the inmates of concentration camps were comfortably accommodated and well fed. Conditions deteriorated, only thanks to the chaos which ensued as the Allied armies moved across Europe. That is what really explains those photographs of emaciated corpses stacked up in piles.

iv in any case, the Jews had declared themselves to be at war with Germany so that they were, in effect, 'the enemy within'.

v the impression that things were otherwise is the outcome of a vast conspiracy orchestrated by communists and – you've guessed it – the Jews.

Some deniers are particularly solicitous towards Hitler's personal reputation, arguing, for example, that

vi Hitler had known nothing of the extermination of the Jews until late in 1943 and that, 'both before and after that had done his best to mitigate the worst anti-Semitic excesses of his subordinates'.

Holocaust deniers prefer to be called 'revisionists' and like to present themselves as serious scholars whose one concern is 'to tell the other side of the story'. There is, for example, a 'Committee for Open Debate on the Holocaust' (CODOH) whose director, one Bradley Smith, first gained notoriety in the 1980s when he placed a full page ad in a number of college newspapers across the United States. The initial ad was headed, 'The Holocaust Story: How Much of it is False?', and promised to answer, 'the questions you've never heard asked'. Another is headed, 'There is no liberty without free speech and open debate', and states, 'Every historical controversy can be debated on national television except one – the jewish holocaust story'. (Note the pointedly lower case 'j'.) Likewise, the UK's David Irving is anxious to emphasize his credibility as a serious historian; that he engages in 'real history' as opposed to the 'Madison-Avenue' and Hollywood versions of history' peddled by his opponents. 'I am the champion of free speech' he claims, 'and I am the champion of Real History'.

These references to 'open debate', 'liberty', 'controversy', 'real history' and – most to the point here – 'free speech', may suggest that Holocaust deniers are advancing a credible, genuinely controversial historical thesis, one which deserve serious consideration. But are they? The question is apposite because, if they were, they would be making a genuine contribution to 'thought and discussion' in the pursuit of truth and their activities would be defensible for the reasons given by Mill. The character of their motives – odious or otherwise – would be beside the point. Against this, I suggest that in reality it would be impossible to sustain the case that they are doing any such thing. This time, the reason is that there can only be some point or purpose to the exercise of discussion where there is genuine room for doubt. But claims (i) – (vi) – that there were no gas chambers, and so on – are incredible claims, so incredible that there is no such room. But don't take my word for it. Rather, let me cite the distinguished (and 'real') historian R.J.Evans, who describes Holocaust denial as 'call[ing] into question a huge mass of historical evidence carefully gathered and interpreted by professional historians over the decades'. (Professor Evans served as an expert witness for the defence in the unsuccessful libel case Irving brought against Deborah Lipstadt, author of *Denying the Holocaust*. You can find his elegant and eloquent, piecemeal deconstruction of Irving's arguments in his *Telling Lies About Hitler*.)

The Irving libel case: In her book, *Denying the Holocaust: The Growing Assault on Truth and Memory*, Deborah Lipstadt describes David Irving as a Holocaust denier. Irving took exception to this, and sued Lipstadt for libel. The case was heard in court in 1996. The judge, Mr Justice Gray, did not accept Irving's claim to be a 'real' historian. In his summing up, he stated that, 'Irving has for his own ideological reasons persistently and deliberately misrepresented and manipulated historical evidence,' and that, 'for the same reasons he has portrayed Hitler in an unwarrantedly favourable light, principally in relation to his attitude towards and responsibility for the treatment of the Jews'.

Two factors are especially likely to obscure the issue here. One is the consideration that it is – of course – perfectly proper that there should be disagreements between historians over the precise course taken by events, including the events of the Nazi era. Accordingly, Holocaust deniers are careful to emphasize their own contribution to such discussions. For example, Irving's work contains contentious reinterpretations of certain key events. For example he argues that on the night of 9–10 November 1938 – aka *Kristallnacht* – when synagogues were burned and Jewish property vandalised right across Germany, Hitler only learnt of these events when they were well under way, and that he then did his best to ameliorate the worst damage. Likewise, Irving's book, *Hitler's War*, contains a detailed, if contentious, account of the Wannsee conference, the meeting at which detailed plans for 'the final solution of the Jewish question' were drawn up. Irving argues that there is no reference to the plan in the conference records, and that it is, therefore, a 'legend' that Hitler ordered the mass killings. Throughout these accounts, there is much reference to telexes, diaries, minutes taken, and the like. All this can look like 'normal' history. However, it does nothing to establish a single item on the list of claims (i) – (vi) as listed above. For example, it would only absolve Hitler of responsibility only with the bizarre assumption that people have no responsibility for events they didn't initiate, even when they subsequently come to occupy positions from which they can control them – as Hitler, being leader of Germany, presumably could.

The second factor is the misconception that, where alternative explanations for a given set of observations are available, all are equally worthy of serious consideration. Consider: It was once put to me that the existence of alien spacecraft, presently circling the Earth, is being concealed from the public by the United States' government. I was assured that the said government is in thrall to the oil industry, that those aliens must be using some pretty amazing fuel with which to power their flying saucers, and that, should its chemical composition be discovered, people might start using it in their cars instead of gasoline. If that were to happen, the oil giants would be put out of business, hence the conspiracy. (I am not making this up! At the time, I was on holiday, and visiting Roswell in New Mexico where aliens are said to have landed back in 1947.)

Now, it is certainly true that, at present, it is impossible to detect any alien spacecraft there may be circling the Earth. However, it is only with the help of some bizarre assumptions that this observations can be used to support the conclusion that the United States' government is concealing their presence in order to protect the oil industry. For example, you would have to assume, not only that spacecraft could circle the Earth with nobody noticing except for the US government, but also that the aliens' space-fuel could actually be used to power the average American automobile. By the same token, while 'normal' historians and Holocaust deniers are agreed upon the absence of a reference to the Final Solution in the Wannsee records, the latter can only absolve Hitler of responsibility by ignoring some very well documented explanations for that absence.

That said, the conclusion warranted here needs to be specified quite carefully. It is *simply* that the theses advanced by Holocaust deniers cannot be regarded as intellectually equivalent to those advanced by serious historians, or as meriting the same attention and respect. For that matter, nor do they merit the same attention as, say, the eye-witness testimony of survivors, the work of documentary film-makers, or the novels of, for example Primo Levi. (In this respect, the claims of Holocaust Denial to be regarded as serious history parallel those of Creationism to be regarded as serious science. Or by analogy, suppose that someone were to attempt a 'slavery denial' thesis, arguing that slavery never really existed in the USA and – for example – that photographs of supposed 'slaves' in the pre-Civil War South had really been taken in Africa. Imagine the enormous revision of the historical record which would have to be undertaken to establish that.) To be specific, Holocaust denial's pretensions to be considered serious history – that is, as making a serious contribution to 'thought and discussion' – cannot be defended with the help of the argument from truth. Pretending that we should spend time defending theses against which there is so much evidence is – as Deborah Lipstadt has put it – pretty much equivalent to arguing that Elvis is alive and well and living in Moscow. This conclusion is worth emphasizing, mainly because Holocaust deniers – anxious to gain media air-time, or to be granted an 'equal platform' with other speakers at college debates – like to present themselves as serious historians. Even so, there may be *other* reasons for debating the theses of Holocaust denial. For example, they may be some 'argument from democracy', similar to those we shall be discussing in the next chapter, from which they may be able to derive some sort of defence – but that's another story.

Who controls the media?

It is obvious that the freedom to pit one's opinions against those of others in open debate, and in the pursuit of truth and understanding, is compromised where a single person, group, or agency, is in such a powerful position that he, she, or it is able to control the debate. That is exactly why absolute, or near-absolute, state control of the media is objectionable. It ought to be equally obvious that the same degree of control is equally objectionable when exerted by a small group of individuals – for example, by a group of press 'barons' whose views on a range of issues are more than likely to be similar.

Obvious though it ought to be, however, the point needs emphasizing thanks to a prevalent fashion for a certain assertively pro-free market rhetoric. For an example, let me draw upon a recent speech by James Murdoch, son of Rupert. (In 2009 he had been invited to give the Edinburgh International Festival's annual James MacTaggart Memorial Lecture, a prestigious event.) In it, Murdoch castigates 'unaccountable institutions like the BBC Trust, Channel Four and Ofcom' and 'excessive regulation' for being 'an infringement of freedom of speech and on the right of people to choose what kind of news to watch'. At the same time, he vaunts the merits of 'genuine independence' in the news media. Murdoch's conclusion is that, 'The only reliable, durable, and perpetual guarantor of independence is profit.' In short, it is Murdoch's thesis that, in a world where the forces of darkness, 'authoritarianism, endless intervention, regulation and control' (aka the BBC) are pitted against 'the free part of the market where success has been achieved by a determined resistance to constant efforts of the authorities to interfere' only the latter can act as the guarantor of independence and free speech.

In fact, this style of rhetoric is so fashionable at present that its worth listing a few reasons for being sceptical of its claims. They include the following: (i) Murdoch's argument confuses the question of *control* with that of *ownership*. I am suggesting, the liberty of thought and discussion can be compromised where a single party is in a position to exert undue control, and that it makes no difference whether that party is the state or a small group of private owners. (ii) Murdoch assumes that, within a free market, originality, innovation, and free speech are fostered even when that market is dominated by a small number of giant corporations. It is as if the twenty-first century media world were comparable to a local market where small-time stallholders compete on roughly equal terms. The assumption is fanciful; (iii) Murdoch assumes that individuals who choose between commodities offered by rival private corporations are, somehow or other, exerting a greater degree of liberty than those who choose between commodities offered by private and publicly run organizations. It is as if, in choosing to buy your cornflakes at Tesco's stores rather than

Morrisons you exercise more liberty than you do when you choose to watch BBC TV rather than Sky. These are big assumptions and, in my view, their flimsy character becomes quite apparent once they are set out in plain English. (And even if you don't agree with me about *that*, you must still recognize that they are assumptions, and need to be defended with argument.)

To this, it is worth adding a comment on Murdoch's repeated references to Darwin; for example, his claims that 'thanks to Darwin we understand that the evolution of a successful species is an unmanaged process' and that, 'Darwin proved that evolution is unmanaged'. We are supposed to conclude that, by analogy, the market works best when left to itself. Such talk may be fashionable, but the trouble with it is that it gets Darwin wrong. In fact, Darwin would never have agreed that the outcome of an 'unmanaged' evolutionary process is necessarily the best for humans. Nor is it true that evolution cannot be 'managed'. The point is recognized, not just by Darwin, but by anyone whose business is the selective breeding of crops or livestock. (To put it another way, if evolution were left to itself, it could turn out that only cockroaches survive, which is great news – but only if you're a cockroach.) Still, I could continue with this theme, but I think I have said enough to suggest that there is no good reason for supposing that a world in which state-sponsored media organizations such as the BBC play a role should be any more inimical to free speech than a market in which a small number of large organizations dominate.

▶ The argument from truth: overview

Role of the discussion group model

The problem cases I have just been discussing form more than a random, 'rag-bag' collection. They are related in two ways. First, each deviates, in one way or another, from 'truth and discussion' considered as an ideal. It is an ideal I represented in the previous chapter with the help of a 'discussion group model'. Second, each reflects the fact that the argument is *consequentialist* in form. Let me take each point in turn.

First, the discussion group model: As I argued in the previous chapter, while this may be artificial, its value lies in its resemblance to other 'real-life' situations. It is, if you like, an 'organizing conception' with the help of which it is possible to make sense of certain familiar claims. If it did nothing else, it would promise a resolution to the ill-conceived and interminable stand-off between 'tough guys' who insist that 'there is no right not to be offended' and 'wimps' who respond with the contention that there is a necessity to respect the sensitivities of certain groups. As for the problem cases, we have already noted that in Southall and Skokie, neither the marchers nor those at whom their hostility is directed could be described, credibly, as confronting each other on equal terms with a view to reaching truth through the exercise of rational discourse. The neo-Nazi spectacular is more than anything else an exercise in hate speech.

Holocaust deniers (like 'slavery deniers') deviate from the model in a different way, by violating the requirement that there should be an issue, genuinely open to doubt and therefore resolvable through rational discussion. Their claim to be advancing a genuinely controversial historical thesis, on a level with other such theses, is thereby invalidated. Finally, the concentration of media control in a few hands is problematic, thanks to the way it deviates from the model's requirement that no-one should be in a position to exert undue influence with a view to determining the outcome of the discussion.

This notion of an organizing conception should be familiar to readers who are at all familiar with political philosophy. The idea of 'the social contract' is another such conception. Elucidated in various ways by the great seventeenth and eighteenth century theorists – Hobbes, Locke and Rousseau – and more recently by the celebrated American philosopher, John Rawls, it supplies a context with which certain claims – for example, that we have 'natural rights' or that we should obey the law unless such-and-such conditions prevail – can be, as it were, intelligibly 'placed'. Of course, it never really happened that prehistoric humans 'signed up' to a contract by which they became morally bound in perpetuity, but that isn't the point of the idea. (Rather, the point is that, by telling a story about why imaginary rational individuals, lacking a political authority to coordinate their activities, would have agreed to establish such an authority, you establish the limits within which an actual authority can legitimately operate.) Likewise, it's possible that the ideal discussion group, comprised of fully rational and dispassionate seekers after truth, could only exist in an imaginary, ideal world. However, that wouldn't prevent it from serving as a useful measuring device.

Finally on this point, and in case it isn't obvious, I should add that the examples I have discussed form a purely illustrative list. There are many others I could have chosen. Just for example, take the notorious *fatwa* issued by Iran's Ayatollah Khomeini against Salman Rushdie in 1988. 'I inform the proud Muslim people of the world,' announced Khomeini, 'that the author of the *Satanic Verses* book which against Islam, the Prophet, and the Koran, and all involved in its publication who were aware of its content, is sentenced to death'. There are *many* reasons for finding Khomeini's pronouncement objectionable. One is that he was interfering with a citizen, and a resident, of a sovereign state other than his own. Another is that death is, in any case, a thoroughly disproportionate 'punishment' to inflict on someone simply for writing a book (or, as in the *Charlie Hebdo* case, for publishing a cartoon, however offensive it may be to some). No doubt, there are others too. But the point here is that it was, amongst other things, a violation of free speech and that the discussion group model can represent it as such by portraying the Ayatollah as attempting to control debate within an arena where individuals who regard each other as equals should be freely exchanging ideas. Moreover, none of this is to mention those who might have joined in, but who chose, through prudence or fear, to remain silent. The model reflects the fact that free speech can be compromised in more than one way.

Consequentialism

The idea that there is a specific form of statement or argument – the consequentialist form – will be perfectly familiar to readers already acquainted with philosophy. It will be less familiar to others, so let me explain, firstly, that a statement is consequentialist if it takes the following form.

Action or activity, A, has consequence, C.

The argument from truth takes this form, for it asserts that thought and discussion (activity A) promotes an increase in the stock of knowledge and understanding available to humanity (consequence C). That might seem obvious to the point of banality, but its implications are – perhaps – not so obvious, so let us now turn to those.

Points to note are as follows: First; you only get a consequentialist *justification* for activity A with the help of the assumption that consequence C has a certain value. In Mill's case, this takes the form of the assumption that there is value in the possession of knowledge and understanding. I have no quarrel with this assumption. After all, we are distinguished from other species by the fact that we are purposive creatures who form plans and projects on the basis of the beliefs we hold. I take it to be obvious that there must be many reasons why we should prefer knowledge to ignorance and understanding to incomprehension. (It's true that Mill has sometimes been criticized for focusing too exclusively on the model of scientific truth, and there may be something in this. After all, he does envisage that, 'As mankind improve, the number of doctrines which are no longer disputed or doubted will be constantly on the increase' and assert that, 'the well-being of mankind may almost be measured by the number and gravity of the truths which have reached the point of being uncontested.' This suggests the degree of certainty which science may strive to attain, but which may well be unattainable in other areas. As I said earlier, that is why I have been careful to speak of knowledge *and understanding* throughout this chapter.)

Second, every consequentialist statement is *contingent* in the sense that its contrary is conceivable. In other words, while it may be true that activity A has consequence C, it might have been the case that it did not. For a start, this means that every consequentialist statement comes with a – usually implicit – exception clause and that, fully spelt out, reads as follows.

> *Action or activity A has consequence C, <u>except when it doesn't</u>.*

You will see what I mean if you compare the foregoing with the necessarily true statement, 'The triangle is a three-sided figure'. To say that a triangle has three sides except when it doesn't is another way of saying that a triangle has three sides except when it isn't a triangle – a world in which some triangles had a number of sides other than three being absolutely *in*conceivable.

Not that this places all consequentialist claims on a level. In some cases, the possibility of their being false is purely hypothetical. As an example, take the statement that the application of heat to water causes it to boil at 100°C (at an atmospheric pressure of 76mm of mercury). This holds true in our corner of the universe, perhaps throughout our universe. It is the expression of a scientifically established law of nature. A world in which different laws applied is, nevertheless, conceivable – which in this case is to say that it is 'imaginable'. (In that other world, but not in this, you might heat up your kettle and find that the water inside has turned to ice.) At the other extreme, there lie consequentialist statements which refer to events or states of affairs which are too specific to instantiate or justify any generalization. As an example, how about this?: 'The slamming of the door startled the waiter into losing his step, dropping his tray, and smashing the crockery'. This may be true in a particular instance, but there is no corresponding generalization from which it derives – i.e. that 'slamming doors startle waiters into losing their step, dropping trays and smashing crockery'.

Now, so what? In answer, I take it that the argument from truth's premise (that where people are left free to argue, discuss, and criticize each other's ideas, the pursuit of knowledge and understanding is usually facilitated) lies closer to the former extreme than it does to the latter. Of course, the possibility that the exercise of thought and discussion will *not* lead to an increase in knowledge and understanding is more than hypothetical. In some cases people will be too stupid or prejudiced for this to happen, or it may be that the questions with which they are concerned are too intractable. (So the possibility does not quite resemble the possibility that water will not boil at 100°C at an atmospheric pressure of 76mm of mercury.) Even so, there are reasons for thinking that the former activity will produce the latter desired consequence *more often than not*, and in this chapter's opening paragraph I outlined some of those reasons – that people will be constrained to rethink their positions, restate their arguments in more careful terms, and so on.

This matters because an argument of principle – an argument which seeks to demonstrate the existence of a *right* to free speech – must show that there is a class of speech acts which ought to be protected *even when the consequences of protecting it – or some of them – are by no means desirable*. Thus, if Holocaust denial represents the exercise of a right to free speech, then it must be demonstrable that it merits protection despite the fact that the consequences of protecting it may turn out to be objectionable. Likewise, if the publication of Edward Snowden's revelations represent the exercise of such a right, then they must be worth publishing despite any threat they may pose to national security.

Let me try to formalize this a little. In the light of the foregoing, I suggest that a persuasive consequentialist argument for the protection of free speech – an 'argument from truth' – would run as follows.

The freedom to perform certain speech acts ought to be protected if:

1 They qualify as instantiating the exercise of 'thought and discussion'.

2 There is a reasonable expectation that they will result in an increase in the amount of knowledge and understanding available to humanity.

and

3 The negative value of their undesirable consequences –
should there be any – is outweighed by the positive
value of the contribution they make to the available
stock of knowledge and understanding.

Note that 'offensive' speech qualifies for protection on
such grounds provided that the negative value of the
offence caused is outweighed by the positive value of
its contribution (potential or actual) to the pursuit of
knowledge and understanding. This seems right. Hate
speech fails to qualify because it satisfies none of criteria
1–3. *OK*'s publication of the 'Cindy Crawford' story fails
because it scarcely satisfies 1 and 2, and therefore fails
to satisfy 3. As for Holocaust denial literature, it scarcely
satisfies 2 – its claims are so patently counterfactual –
and therefore fails to satisfy 3. But, if I am right, the
exercise of thought and discussion satisfies all three
criteria *in most cases*. If I am right, then, it *is* possible
to frame a credible consequentialist argument for the
liberty of thought and discussion while at the same time
placing problem cases into perspective

Now, I realize that the analysis of an argument at the
structural level, characteristic of philosophy, may not
be to everyone's taste, but without it we are in danger
of remaining oblivious to pitfalls, in this case to the
traps lying in wait for anyone seeking to construct a
consequentialist defence of free speech. By way of an
example, take a claim drawn from a recent book by
Nick Cohen, according to whom, 'Few liberals have the
confidence to say that free speech, like sexual freedom,

would not create a terrible society, because they do not trust their fellow citizens'. According to Cohen, 'They do not realise that most people in modern democracies do not harbour secret fascist fantasies, and that the best way to respond to those who do is to meet their bad arguments with better arguments'. Note that Cohen's argument is consequentialist, and that it rests upon a claim of fact which is open to empirical test and which may turn out to be false. The claim is that, where people are prey to fascist sympathies, those sympathies can be dispelled through exposure to open debate and rational critique. I would like him to be right, but, as a European, I am all too well aware that racism, xenophobia, fear of 'the other' and mystical ultra-nationalism – the attitudes and ideas which characterize fascism – lurk throughout the culture, and that they may easily surface, especially in times of economic recession. They are, perhaps, not so easily conjured away. (That apart, I can't resist pointing out, contrary to Cohen, that exercising free speech is probably quite a poor technique for ridding people of 'secret fascist fantasies'. Don't these involve, for example, dressing up in weird uniforms for kinky sexual purposes and aren't they best treated by psychotherapy?)

▶ Conclusions

From thought and discussion to free speech?

In conclusion, it should be clear that the argument from truth is limited in scope. The assumption upon which it is premised – that, where people are left free to argue and discuss, their chances of acquiring knowledge and understanding are greatly increased – may be true enough, but the upshot of my discussion is that it cannot be generalized to cover all cases in which free speech is often thought be at issue. The news is not all bad, however. The reverse side to this particular coin is the conclusion that the argument from truth, correctly understood, does provide a convincing defence of some activities, and especially the activities which those who insist that 'there is no right not to be offended' are especially concerned to protect. At any rate, it does so provided that the expression 'thought and discussion' is construed broadly to include, not just what goes on (ideally) in an academic seminar – where ideas framed in sentences are literally pitted against each other for critical examination – but in literature for example, 'the one place in any society where, within the secrecy of our own heads, we can hear voices talking about everything in every possible way' (as Salman Rushdie puts it) or in the expression of a proposition or attitude through the production of images – satirical cartoons or *Guernica*.

It would be wrong to exaggerate the significance of this conclusion. So far, I have said nothing from which it follows that any of the problematic activities I have discussed should be proscribed by law. There remain two possibilities. One the one hand, there may be arguments of principle, other than the argument from truth from which it follows that neo-Nazis, Holocaust deniers, and the like have a right to free speech. On the other, there may be good reasons why the activities of such individuals should be tolerated – but reasons are purely pragmatic and not founded upon principle.

Mill and the spirit of his age

Had Mill been alive today, and were he to read this chapter, what would he have made of it? Well, here is a passage from 'The Spirit of the Age', an essay he published in 1831.

> *Men may not reason better, concerning the great questions in which human nature is interested, but they reason more. Large subjects are discussed more, and longer, and by more minds. Discussion has penetrated deeper into society; and if no greater numbers than before have attained the higher degrees of intelligence, fewer grovel in that state of abject stupidity, which can only co-exist with utter apathy and sluggishness.*

Mill is reflecting upon the differences between his own time and that of the previous generation, the generation of his father, James Mill, and their joint utilitarian mentor, Jeremy Bentham. They were huge differences. The earlier generation had witnessed the French Revolution, the Napoleonic wars, and the political and economic turmoil of the post-Napoleonic period. The intervening period had witnessed industrialization and, with it, the rise of a sizeable working and lower middle class. This most numerous class had changed its character. It was no longer the insurrectionary rabble so feared by the ruling class. (In the earlier period, the Duke of Wellington, Tory Prime Minister, had berated the new-fangled railways for encouraging 'the lower orders to go uselessly wandering about the country'. He hadn't been kidding.) It had been replaced by a new working/middle class whose members were, in the main, sober, hard-working, thrifty, conscious of their 'respectability', conscientiously religious and, most of all oppressively conformist. The role of 'discussion' had been to expedite the breakdown of old prejudices and facilitate the march of progress. But it also had another role, that of serving as an antidote to the conformist 'tyranny of the majority' – the 'tyranny of the prevailing opinion and feeling' – which threatened to engulf society.

I should like to think that Mill would have recognized my 'discussion group model' as more or less representing what he had in mind when he wrote of 'thought and discussion'. As for details, there are passages in Mill's work which suggest that Mill would have been happy to place restrictions on hate speech. For example, there is another essay, 'Law of Libel and the Liberty of the Press', in which he states, 'That the press may be so employed as to require punishment, we are very far from denying', and that, 'it may be made the instrument of almost every imaginable crime'. Elsewhere, however, there are lines which suggest that he would have been less restrictive.

Still, this chapter has been an exercise in philosophy, and my aim has been to elucidate his position with arguments which are faithful to its spirit if not of every letter of its text. One thing the passage does make clear is that, for Mill, 'discussion' served as part of an ideal to which society may conform in a greater or a lesser degree. That is, he held that society at large – its major institutions, the way they are organized and operated – should aspire to resemble an arena within which genuine 'thought and discussion' can be conducted. In my view, this is an inspiring ideal – provided that one construes 'thought and discussion' broadly, of course. It is an ideal which has continued to play a major role in the development of thought about free speech.

Free speech and democracy

In his 1948 essay, *Free Speech and Its Relation to Self-Government*, Alexander Meiklejohn paints the following portrait of the typical American town meeting.

> *In the town meeting the people of a community assemble to discuss and act upon matters of public interest – roads, schools, poorhouses, health, external defence, and the like. Every man is free to come. They meet as political equals. Each has a right and a duty to think his own thoughts, to express them, and to listen to the arguments of others. The basic principle is that freedom of speech shall be unabridged. And yet, the meeting cannot even be opened unless, by common consent, speech is abridged. A chairman, or moderator is, or has been chosen. He 'calls the meeting to order'. And the hush which follows that call is a clear indication that restrictions on speech have been set up.*

In other words, while there are procedures to be followed – while 'the meeting cannot even be opened unless, by common consent, speech is abridged' – there must be no restriction upon the *content* of what is said. Thus, ...

> *But however it be arranged, the vital point, as stated negatively, is that no suggestion of policy shall be denied a hearing because it is on one side of the issue rather than another. And this means that though citizens may, on other grounds, be barred from speaking, they may not be barred because their views are thought to be false or dangerous. No plan of action shall be outlawed because someone*

in control thinks it unwise, unfair, un-American. No speaker may be declared 'out of order' because we disagree with what he intends to say.

▲ 'Freedom of Speech' by Norman Rockwell

I have never attended an American town meeting, but I'm inclined to think that Meiklejohn's account is more than a little sentimentalized. It is too redolent of Norman Rockwell's famous cover illustrations for *The Saturday Evening Post*. With that in mind, I ought start by pointing out, in Meiklejohn's defence, that there is political critique implicit within his description of the meeting. For one thing, one of his targets is Justice Wendell Holmes's doctrine that free speech may be suppressed in circumstances which are 'of such a nature as to create a clear and present danger that they will bring about the substantive evils that Congress has a right to prevent'. We discussed this briefly in chapter one. (Precisely what counts as a 'clear and present danger' is, of course, a matter of judgement, and the doctrine could easily be used by repressive regimes to suspend democracy itself.) For another, Meiklejohn – a prominent scholar and an active member of the American Civil Liberties Union – was writing at a time when the infamous Senator Joe McCarthy was continuing to persecute publicly prominent individuals for their allegedly 'un-American activities'. He was well aware that Inquisition-style heresy-hunting could take place, even in the United States of the twentieth century. The target of his insistence that, 'No plan of action shall be outlawed because someone in control thinks it unwise, unfair, *un-American'* would have been immediately recognizable to his contemporaries.

But then, idealization is not the point. Even if Meiklejohn's account of the meeting were completely fictitious, it would still serve its intended purpose as, 'a model by which free political procedures may be measured'. That is because Meiklejohn intends the town meeting to exemplify self-government in action, and self-government is, he holds, the ideal which the United States' Constitution was designed to embody and protect. The purpose of his description is to emphasize that the ideal cannot be realized in the absence of the liberty affirmed by the Constitution's First Amendment, so, for the benefit of readers who are not US citizens and who may not be so familiar with the amendment, here it is.

> *Congress shall make no law respecting an establishment of religion, or prohibiting the free exercise thereof; or abridging the freedom of speech, or of the press; or of the right of the people peaceably to assemble, and to petition the government for a redress of grievances.*

For our purposes, the amendment's relevant feature is – of course – its emphasis upon freedom of speech and the press, not its prohibition of established religion.

There are obvious similarities between the situation idealized by Mill, in which individuals enjoy an unrestricted liberty of thought and discussion, and Meiklejohn's idealized town meeting. Thus, each pictures a situation in which individuals who confront each other as equals engage in discussion with a view to reaching informed judgements. This can make it easy to overlook the differences. Notice then that, whereas Mill grounds the value of discussion in that of truth and, thereby, in that of progress, on Meiklejohn's account discussion derives its impetus from the need to achieve consensus upon plans of action – or, as he puts it at one point, to vote 'wise decisions'.

Meiklejohn's is *just one* example of an argument which seeks to account for the value of free speech by connecting it with the value of democracy. That is the connection I propose to explore in this chapter. The task is complicated by the fact that the definition of the term 'democracy' is itself highly contentious. Accordingly, the role played by free speech in the democratic process has also been described in a number of contrasting ways. Here, I shall focus upon just two theoretical accounts of democracy. One, I shall term the 'force-field' view. The other advocates 'deliberative democracy'. (I take Meiklejohn's account to be a version of the latter, and we shall be turning to it later in the chapter.)

▶ What is democracy?: Why does it matter?

Before I turn to either account, however, I ought to say something in answer to the above questions. It's not that I intend to digress or change the subject. It's just that we need some idea of the phenomenon we are dealing with. In this section, then, I shall suggest two criteria which any political system must satisfy if it is to qualify as a democracy. These are (i) the existence of voting somewhere in the system and (ii) that it must qualify as 'rule by the people', in some sense of that porous expression. (These are, in the jargon, *necessary conditions* for a system's being a democracy, although they may not be sufficient conditions.) I shall then distinguish two different categories of justification to which democracy is open; that is, two different ways of arguing that democracy is preferable to other systems.

Voting

I think readers will agree that, the way the term 'democracy' is generally understood, voting must take place within the system if it is to qualify as genuinely democratic. At least, I believe – and hope – they will agree. Moreover, the voting system must be of a kind which actually determines outcomes – the make-up of a government, future policy, the membership of committees, and so on. That is why a purely consultative system cannot be counted a democracy. By a consultative system, I mean one in which the ruler draws upon a certain group, such as the membership of a convened assembly, for advice and support – advice which he or she need not take, and support which may be gained elsewhere. (Examples would be the English parliament of the medieval period or the French Estates-General in the years preceding the revolution of 1789.) While the latter may render government *responsive* to popular demand, it does not treat that demand as *decisive*.

Something must hang on the extent of the franchise, of course. For example, it is both conceivable and likely that, in the day-to-day operation of a military dictatorship, committees of generals will sometimes reach decisions by taking votes. Even so, a ruling military junta is, by definition, not a democracy. On the other hand, however, the system which flourished in Athens in the 5th and 4th centuries BCE certainly was a democracy – or so it is generally agreed – and that is despite the fact that only male citizens were entitled to participate in the assembly and vote. (Women, slaves, and resident aliens –

altogether a sizeable proportion of the population – were excluded.) Likewise, it seems right to describe the UK, prior to 1928, as having been a democracy, even though it was only in that year that women gained the same voting rights as men. How wide must the franchise be, then, before a system can be counted a democracy? It's an important question but, fortunately for me, my subject is free speech, so I shall set it to one side.

Rule by the people

As I am sure readers will also agree, the definition of democracy as 'rule by the people' is minimally informative. Pretty much everything hangs upon who 'the people' are supposed to be. In 4th century BCE Greece, democracy was understood to be rule by the *demos*, that is, the ordinary citizens. Plato's dialogue, the *Republic*, thus contains a famous section in which he contrasts democracy with timarchy, oligarchy, and tyranny; that is – respectively – rule by an aristocratic military élite, by a small group of powerful, wealthy individuals, and subjection to the arbitrary will of ruthless individuals. It is a fourfold classification which distinguishes regimes in terms of the group, or class, in whose hands power is placed in each. Alternatively, you might take 'the people' to include every member of the community, and dismiss considerations of gender, age, wealth, social class, educational qualification, and so on, as irrelevant. (It is, thus, Meiklejohn's argument that *anyone* is entitled to attend the town meeting.) Or again, prior to the collapse of the Berlin Wall in 1989, the one-party regimes of eastern Europe described themselves as 'people's' democracies on the grounds that the party was the true representative of the proletariat, that is, the revolutionary working class. In short, the expression 'rule by the people' is wide open to interpretation. Of course, some of these interpretations are more persuasive than others, but it would be beside the point to consider their relative merits here.

In his dialogue, *The Republic*, the Greek philosopher Plato (427–347 BCE) expresses extreme hostility to the idea of democracy. 'A democratic society in its thirst for liberty' he said, 'may fall under the influence of bad leaders, who intoxicate it with excessive quantities of the neat spirit'. He may have a point. At any rate, even a fervent democrat would find it hard to disagree with him that the most popular leaders are not necessarily the best.

Two modes of justification

What makes democracy preferable to other forms of government (assuming that it is)? Answers to the question have tended to fall into one or the other of two categories. Some purport to show that democracy is the system which operates in a way most likely to bring about certain *desirable outcomes*. A utilitarian argument purporting to show that democracy is most likely to bring about 'the greatest happiness of the greatest number' would fall into this category. Alternatively, you might try to show that democracy produces the best decisions in some less exalted sense of 'the best'. For example, you might agree with Karl Popper that democracy's great virtue lies in the way it enables the electorate to dispense with bad leaders before they can do too much damage, or with Winston Churchill that, 'democracy is the worst form of government except for all the others that have been tried'.

By contrast, arguments which fall into the second category purport to show that democratically arrived-at decisions carry a *legitimacy* others lack; in other words, that individuals who are disinclined to abide by those decisions are, nevertheless under a moral obligation to do so. (In a democracy, this normally means that, after a vote has been taken, the minority should respect the expressed will of the majority.) Note that these arguments focus upon *the way laws originate* rather than upon their content or the outcome of their operation. They constitute one solution – 'the democratic solution' – to a problem which is sometimes known as, 'the problem of political obligation'. Others are the Socratic solution ('You must always obey the law, however it is passed and however absurd it may be'); the argument from divine right ('you must obey the monarch because the monarch is God's representative on Earth'); and the anarchist solution ('there is no such thing as a moral obligation to obey the law'). It would be interesting to pursue these claims, but it's now time to get back to the main subject.

To summarize, the points I have been making in this section are as follows: Whatever else it may be, democracy is a (i) political system in whose operation voting plays a decisive role *at certain points*, and (ii) is 'rule by the people' *in some sense of that expression*. It may be argued that democracy is preferable to other systems either (iii) on the grounds that it is the one more likely to produce certain *desirable outcomes*, or (iv) on the grounds that decisions which are democratically arrived at carry a *legitimacy* others lack. That may yield a pretty minimal specification, but it is enough to supply a standard against which to measure the models of democracy we shall now be going on to discuss.

▶ The force-field model

In the concluding section of his influential essay, *A Preface to Democratic Theory*, the American political scientist, R.A.Dahl, summarizes the weaknesses and strengths of the American political system, as he takes them to be. He writes:

> [I]t is a markedly decentralized system. Decisions are made by endless bargaining; perhaps in no other national political system in the world is bargaining so basic a component of the political process.

And:

> Luckily the normal system has the virtues of its vices. With all its defects, it does nonetheless provide a high probability that any active and legitimate group will make itself heard effectively at some stage in the process of decision. This is no mean thing in a political system.

For our purposes, two features of Dahl's conclusion are noteworthy. The first is that it is drawn from the application of what he calls 'the descriptive method'.

This, he describes as 'consider[ing] as a single class of phenomena all those nation states and social organizations that are commonly called democratic by political scientists', with a view to determining their distinguishing characteristics and 'the necessary and sufficient conditions for their organization'. This is just one respect in which Dahl's book – first published in 1956 – typifies the pragmatic, empiricistic turn which was taken by political theory in the decades immediately following World War Two. You will see what I mean if you consider the obvious contrast between Dahl and – say – Plato, whose *Republic* contains a description of an ideal state; one which is non-existent, but which is intended to set a pattern to which actual states should strive to conform. You could say that, by contrast with Plato, Dahl is trying to describe things as they really are, rather than as they might be.

It is equally noteworthy, secondly, that Dahl's conclusion rests upon the assumption that society – in this case American society – is fundamentally, inescapably, plural. That is to say, society is portrayed as comprising a wide and diverse variety of groups, each placing its own demands upon the democratic system, and the system itself as a sort of input-output machine tasked with processing those demands and yielding an outcome which is more or less responsive to them. As he puts it, they 'make themselves heard effectively' – hence my epithet, 'the force-field model'.

At this point, I should explain that Dahl is by no means the only writer to have represented society in this way. The model has a distinguished ancestry in the work of – for example – the US Constitution's founding fathers, and especially in that of Dahl's mentor, James Madison. Madison insisted that the Constitution should include *checks* against 'tyranny', which he defined as 'the accumulation of all powers, legislative, executive, and judiciary, in the same hands, whether of one, a few, or many'. The idea that society is an arena within which differing groups each seek to further their conflicting 'interests' also plays a central role in the work of the nineteenth century Utilitarians, James Mill, Jeremy Bentham, and John Stuart Mill. As for Dahl himself, while his *Preface* was published some years ago, he continued to work on democracy throughout his life, and his most recent work on the subject was published in 2006.

In short, the 'force-field' view of society – and, with it, an 'input-output' model of democracy – is ubiquitously held these days. Dahl's is just one version of that view, of course – albeit an exceptionally clear and well-articulated version – and we may treat it as representative. Moreover, in addition to being representative of an academic trend, Dahl's is one version of a 'received' view. At least, I think it is, for I am pretty sure that, while at school or college, many readers will have been presented with the idea that, essentially, democracy is a system for responding to the demands of groups – 'pressure' groups, 'interest' groups, and the like – as if it were the plain truth. In fact, my guess is that some readers will be surprised by my suggestion that the force-field model is, as I am calling it, a 'model'. But it is, if only in the sense that it selects certain features of contemporary society for attention, and not others.

The role played by free speech in Dahl's scenario

What are we to make of this, and – especially – how should we evaluate the role free speech must play within the context of Dahl's scenario? In seeking an answer, I suggest that we consider how his account measures up to the standards I established in the previous section and, for our purposes, the crucial item on the list is the first, namely voting. A moment ago, I argued that, if a system is to qualify as a democracy then, as a minimally necessary condition, it must be the case that voting is treated as decisive at some point in its operation. Here, voting is crucial because, within the context of Dahl's scenario, the roles played by voting and that played by the exercise of free speech must be closely analogous.

Recall that, so far as Dahl is concerned, the great virtue of the US system is that it 'provides a high probability that citizen group[s] will make [themselves] heard effectively at some stage in the process of decision'. Here, the point is that, at any one time, there may be – and usually are – *many* available methods for exerting an influence on the latter process. The vote is *just one*. Others may include participating in local committees, writing to the newspaper, participating in public demonstrations, getting up a petition, posting one's opinions on the internet (blogging), and so on. The full list is long and changing. Dahl would agree and, indeed, if the whole point is that citizens should be able to exercise such an influence, one wonders why he should think it necessary that there should be elections at all – at least, not when there are so many other means available to citizens. (He does, however, describing the electoral process as a fundamental method of social control, which 'make[s] governmental leaders so responsive to non-leaders that the distinction between democracy and dictatorship still makes sense'. This is, presumably, an empirically based claim. It may be true, but we needn't consider it here.)

Now, to turn from the vote to the exercise of free speech, it should be clear that Dahl must also portray the latter as a means of exerting an influence upon the decision-making process – of inputting a preference, if you like. (As he occasionally puts it, 'freedom of speech' is 'a key prerequisite to political equality and popular sovereignty'.) Not that he is wrong. On the contrary, the truth in this representation is obvious. Thus, in the period between elections, and where there is a free press, it is just routine that newspapers of all political stripes should propagandize and campaign with a view to changing the political course of events. Some of the other activities I mentioned just now – demonstrating, petitioning, blogging, and so on – must also qualify as exercising the right to free speech with a view to effecting such changes. As for election times themselves, it would be hard to imagine an election campaign in which newspaper campaigns, leaflets, posters on hoardings – etcetera – did not play an integral role.

The role of rationality

But if so much is plain obvious, it only means that, if we are to appreciate the distinctive character of the force field model, we should concentrate not so much upon what it can accommodate, but upon what it rules out. One example of a claim ruled out by the force-field model is, thus, the claim that the outcome of an election expresses 'the general will' or 'the will of the people'. The best known formulation of this claim, by far, is Jean Jacques Rousseau's. Here is how he put it in *The Social Contract* (1762).

> *When a law is proposed in the people's assembly, what is asked of them is not precisely whether they approve of the proposition or reject it, but whether it is in conformity with the general will, which is theirs; each by giving his vote gives his opinion on this question, and the counting of votes yields a declaration of the general will.*

In fact, there are many reasons for being sceptical of Rousseau's claim. For example, it's hard to see how one can talk of 'the people's will' without invoking the existence of a mysterious super-person – 'the people' – with a will of its own, and distinct from the individual flesh-and-blood people who actually vote; and it's difficult to see how one could do that without lapsing into fiction. But, for our purposes, it is important to set such objections to one side and appreciate the specific reason for which the claim in question is ruled out by the force-field model. This lies with the latter's assumption that a realistic account must recognize that modern society is characterized by plurality at a fundamental level; in other words, that there is *no more to the story than that*. If this is right, then it *cannot* be true that there is some over-riding 'general will' into which the claims of competing individuals and groups can be incorporated.

It is equally noteworthy that, rather as talk of a general will is ruled out by the force-field model, so rationality is assigned a relatively minor role; 'relatively minor', that is, in comparison with the role it plays in John Stuart Mill's defence of the liberty of thought and discussion or, indeed, in Meiklejohn's account of the town meeting. Thus, in the case of Mill's argument, rationality is – you could say – the motor which drives the quest for knowledge and understanding in the right direction. I mean that, where differing opinions are brought into 'collision', it follows that the pursuit of truth will be facilitated thereby, only if it is also the case that the individuals who hold those opinions are prepared to test them against known standards of reason and evidence. Otherwise anything could be the outcome. Emotion and prejudice might easily win the day. Similarly, at Meiklejohn's idealized town meeting, people 'meet as political equals. Each has a right and a duty to think his own thoughts, to express them, and to listen to the arguments of others'. In short, it has to be assumed that sober, ordered, rationality is the rule. If it were not, their chances of reaching 'wise decisions' would be nullified.

By contrast, no such restriction is imposed upon freedom of speech by the force-field model. That is because it portrays the latter as, essentially, a vehicle for the expression of preferences. Here, the point is that, while preferences may be more or less rationally held, they needn't be. It is true that on one hand, an intelligent voter might assess the issues and the policies on offer and conclude that such-and-such a party is the one to vote for. That would be an example of a rationally formed preference. But then, a 'brute' taste such as a liking for strawberry ice-cream rather than vanilla is also a preference, although you could hardly say that it's formed on the basis of a rational judgement. Between these extremes there lie many intermediate possibilities including, crucially, the preferences, which motivate voters at election times.

One of Dahl's contemporaries, Joseph Schumpeter, took an extremely cynical view of the latter. '[T]he typical citizen drops down to a lower level of mental performance as soon as he enters the political field,' he wrote. 'He argues and analyses in a way he would readily recognize as infantile within the sphere of his real interests. He becomes a primitive again. His thinking becomes associative and affective, and, 'simply because he is not "all there", he will relax his usual moral standards as well and occasionally give in to dark urges'. I leave it to you, the reader, to judge the accuracy of this depressing picture of voting behaviour.

On this point, note, finally, that this diminution of rationality's role reflects one of the force-field model's structural features. In other words, it is no accident. It arises from the fact that the model must portray the exercise of free speech as just one method amongst others for exerting an influence upon the decision-making process. One might choose to write to the paper, for example, but then there might be circumstances in which pushing a button would do just as well. The fact that there is a specifically linguistic element to the exercise of free speech is thereby underplayed – inevitably so.

Evaluating the force-field model

The force-field model's aspirations to credibility are rooted in its claim to be realistic – 'realistic' in the sense that it presents an accurate portrait of modern society, considered at a most fundamental level. So, is it? In answer, consider – firstly – the two minimally necessary conditions which, as I argued earlier, any system must satisfy if it is to qualify as democratic. The first was that voting must be treated as decisive at some point in the system's operation. We have already considered the manner in which the force-field model of democracy meets this criterion. The second was that there must be some sense of the expression in which the system can be said to exemplify, 'rule by the people'. On this point, it could be argued that democracy, as construed by the model, does exemplify rule by the people, if only in the sense that it provides a widespread opportunity, on the part of numerous groups, to exert an influence upon decision making. Anything more ambitious, or 'just' is ruled out. For example, the idea that each group's opportunity to exert the latter influence might be equal to that of the others is discounted as unrealistic.

Now recall my distinction between two forms of argument for the conclusion that democracy is preferable to other systems. Arguments of one form purport to show that democracy, in the way it operates, is more likely than other systems to yield such-and-such desirable outcomes. Arguments of the other represent the democratic process as conferring legitimacy upon the decisions it yields. Here, it should be clear that the justification of democracy advanced by the force-field model falls firmly into the former camp. At least it does if you think, as it is reasonable to, that enabling numerous groups to exert an influence on the decision-making process is itself a desirable outcome, and – agreeing with Dahl that the system is conducive to stability – you also think that stability is desirable. As for the latter form, a defence of democracy in such terms is ruled out by the model's emphasis upon 'realism' with its corresponding rejection of 'fancy' metaphysical conceptions such as, 'the general will'.

Now, I haven't forgotten that my subject is, specifically, free speech, and not democracy *per se*. If I've given the wrong impression, that is because the features I've just been describing – the way pressure is exerted on the decision-making process through interest groups, and so on – are manifested in many ways throughout the system. There is nothing specific to the exercise of free speech about them. This is inevitable in fact because, as noted, the model portrays free speech as just one method amongst others for exerting an influence upon political decisions. In this respect, and as also noted, it differs from accounts which emphasize free speech's distinctively linguistic features – the use of argument in an appeal to the rational judgement of others, for example. So far as the model is concerned, while influence upon the system may sometimes be exerted linguistically, at others it may equally well be exercised through a vote or with the click of a mouse. This means that, when assessed, the force-field model's account of free speech must stand or fall with the model considered as a whole.

With that in mind, then, let us return to the question at hand, which is; how realistic is the force-field model's description of modern democracy? On that score, my guess is that many readers will think it extremely realistic. Perhaps they will be attracted by its commonsensical, no-nonsense approach – its disdain for abstraction. Perhaps, some will be attracted by the 'Schumpeterian variant', as I suppose I should call it. By this, I mean Joseph Schumpeter's argument that, when elections are held, parties compete for votes in exactly the way that firms compete for customers within a market context. Language plays a role here, but as a means to promote 'electoral packages' in just the way it is used by advertisers to sell anything else.

Nevertheless, there are reasons to be cautious here. One is that the force-field model is just that – a model – and, like any description, it must single out certain features for attention at the expense of others. There remains the possibility of there being something it has missed. Another is that, as advice, 'Be Realistic!' is ambiguous. It can mean, 'Make sure you take an accurate view of things'. Alternatively, it can be taken to mean, 'Don't let your hopes run too high'. Arguably, the latter advice is implicit in, say, Dahl's decision to treat the status quo as definitive of democracy, that is, 'to consider as a single class of phenomena all those nation states and social organizations that are commonly called democratic by political scientists' and to elucidate their common characteristics. It is an approach which precludes the possibility of selecting some other – perhaps more inspiring – model of democracy, and using it as a standard against which to measure currently existing systems. This could be seen as a counsel of despair, guaranteed to lower expectations.

▶ Deliberative democracy

The arguments I have been discussing up to this point have tended to focus upon democracy's 'procedural' features; that is, upon the fact that it is distinguishable from systems of government by the manner in which decisions are reached and laws established. But that is not the only way to think of democracy, and some writers have tended to focus, rather, upon the idea that a 'democratic society' is characterized, and rendered distinctive, by the relationship of equality which holds between its citizens. It is this feature which informs the work of, for example, Alexis de Tocqueville, the eighteenth century French aristocrat, who opens his famous work, *Democracy in America*, by remarking that, 'Of all the novel things which attracted my attention during my stay in the United States, none struck me more forcibly than the equality of social conditions'. Invoking a similar vision, though more recently, John Rawls has observed that, 'The political culture of a democratic society is always marked by a diversity of opposing and irreconcilable religious, philosophical, and moral doctrines', and – accordingly – formulated 'the problem of political liberalism' as follows: '[H]ow is it possible for there to exist over time a just and stable society of free and equal citizens, who remain profoundly divided by reasonable religious, philosophical, and moral doctrines.'

Equally recently, some political theorists and philosophers have set out to defend a conception of 'deliberative democracy'. The following passage, which is drawn from Amy Gutmann and Dennis Thompson's *Democracy and Disagreement*, should give you an idea of what is at stake here. (Unsurprisingly, there are many differences between the versions of deliberative democracy presented by the writers in this group, but I shall treat Gutmann and Thompson's work as representative.)

> *Deliberative democracy asks citizens and officials to justify public policy by giving reasons that can be accepted by those who are bound by it. This disposition to seek mutually justifiable reasons expresses the core of the process of deliberation. More specifically, the disposition implies three principles – reciprocity, publicity, and accountability – ...... Each addresses an aspect of the reason-giving process: the kind of reasons that should be given, the forum in which they should be given, and the agents to whom and by whom they should be given. Reciprocity is the leading principle because it shapes the meaning of publicity and accountability and also influences the interpretation of liberty and opportunity.*

This is an attractive vision. Rationally disposed individuals are portrayed as confronting each other as equals within an arena in which each must explain and justify his or her most considered judgements to the others. Likewise, officials must be transparent in their reasoning and publicly accountable. It also supplies a contrast with the 'force-field' vision of a world in which individuals and groups compete, each with the others, in an endeavour to satisfy 'interests'.

But why discuss it here, in the context of a book whose subject is supposed to be free speech? The answer is that, unlike the force-field view, deliberative democracy attaches a special role to argument and the exchange of ideas. Put it this way: As I argued earlier (in chapter one) an account of free speech must single out a class of 'speech acts' and explain why such acts merit special protection. An example discussed in chapter two, is Mill's defence of 'the liberty of thought and discussion' which singles out speech acts likely to facilitate the pursuit of knowledge and understanding. Another example is the force-field account of democracy. This singles out 'speech acts' which enable one group or another to exert an influence on the decision-making process. By the same token, deliberative democracy places a special protective cordon around 'deliberative speech' (as I suppose one should call it). It is, therefore, an example of a thesis which seeks to explain the value of free speech by connecting it with that of democracy.

What, then, should we make of it? Space is limited, so – in answer – let me concentrate upon just three questions which are especially relevant to this book's subject. They are: (i) What is 'deliberation'?; (ii) What is its outcome meant to be?; (iii) How realistic is deliberative democracy's vision of the good society?

What is 'deliberation'?

It is easier to describe what deliberation is *not*, than to explain what it is. Thus, if the parties to an argument were unduly swayed by emotion or hysteria, they would not be engaged in deliberation; at least, not as the latter tends to be portrayed by advocates of deliberative democracy. There is, thus, a famous passage in which John Stuart Mill writes, 'An opinion that corn-dealers are starvers of the poor, or that private property is robbery, ought to be unmolested when simply circulated through the press, but may justly incur punishment when delivered orally to an excited mob assembled before the house of a corn-dealer, or when handed about among the same mob in the form of a placard.' One difference between the two situations Mill distinguishes (circulating an opinion through the press and delivering it orally to an excited mob) – or so one might argue – is that, whereas the former can be counted an exercise in 'deliberation', the latter cannot.

Again, deliberation is not bargaining; that is, it cannot be compared with – for example – the negotiation in which economic agents, acting within the context of a free market, typically engage. Bargaining takes place when self-interested parties, each in pursuit of their own ends, strike up compromises. On the contrary, parties engaged in deliberation may appeal to many considerations, moral as well as pragmatic. They may appeal to values such as 'the good of the community' or 'the prospects for world peace'. As Gutmann and Thompson put it, 'Mutual justification means not merely offering reasons to other people, or even offering reasons that they happen to accept (for example, because they are in a weak bargaining position). It means providing reasons that constitute a justification for imposing binding laws on them'.

But if those are situations in which deliberation is remarkable only for its absence, what then is it? We should conclude – I suppose – that deliberation must involve reasoned debate between reflective individuals in a relatively calm atmosphere. But is that all there is to it? Should we conclude that deliberative democracy amounts to nothing more than the platitudinous thesis that reasoned debated is preferable to hysterical screeching or self-serving argy-bargy? I think not, and to see why let us now turn to the following question.

What is the outcome of deliberation supposed to be?

In the literature of deliberative democracy, the outcome of deliberation is variously characterized. For example, and as noted, Alexander Meiklejohn thinks that deliberation at the town meeting is more likely than not to result in 'wise decisions'. He also describes the meeting as 'self-government in its simplest form' (the self-government in question being, supposedly, the self-government enshrined in the US constitution). Taking a different tack, Gutmann and Thompson argue that, 'Reciprocity holds that citizens owe one another justifications for the mutually binding laws and public policies they collectively enact', and that, 'The aim of a theory that takes reciprocity seriously is to help people seek political agreement on the basis of principles that can be justified to others who share the aim of reaching such an agreement'. The outcome of deliberation is, thus, meant to be that decisions are reached which can be seen as 'justified', even by those who disagree with those decisions.

There are questions about just how credible, or even coherent, these claims are. For example, to take Meiklejohn first, it is reasonable to think that those who attend the town meeting will arrive – most of them – with their opinions fully formed, as they will with 'interests' deriving from their membership of various groups. Why suppose that any subsequent discussion will result in consensus, or in decisions which are any more wise? On the contrary, there are reasons for thinking that, where people are forced to defend a view they already hold against the arguments of others, they will simply find better reasons for holding the former. In short, their opinions may become still more entrenched. On the other hand, should it transpire that consensus *is* achieved, this may simply mean that radical views have been marginalised and conformity encouraged. It was, after all, 'the tyranny of the majority' by which de Tocqueville considered democracy to be most threatened.

All this suggests that Meiklejohn's scenario rests upon empirical claims which could well turn out to be false. As for Gutmann and Thompson's argument that, ideally, deliberation should result in 'agreement on the basis of principles that can be justified to others who share the aim of reaching such an agreement', it could be that their suggestion is incoherent. Consider the case of two deliberating individuals, P and Q. Suppose that P argues that because (i) every person is equally deserving of concern and respect, it is (ii) wrong that people should be forcibly deprived of their hard-earned wealth for ends deemed to be good by others and therefore (iii) that proposals for the introduction of a taxpayer-funded health care system should be rejected. Suppose that Q argues, against this, that because (i-a) every person deserves the opportunity to live a minimally decent life it is (ii-a) wrong that some people should be so disadvantaged, thanks to the operation of market forces, that they cannot afford health care and therefore (iii-a) that proposals for the introduction of a taxpayer-funded health care system should be supported. In short, suppose that P is a 'neo-liberal' supporter of *laisser-faire* and the free market, whereas Q is a proponent of socially conscious Keynesian interventionism. Finally, suppose that there is soon to be a vote on whether to adopt the proposal to introduce a taxpayer-funded health care system.

Now ask, is it possible that, out of P and Q, each can regard the other's position as *justified*? I think that this is a possibility, but only in the sense that each can regard the other's position as *rationally founded*. That is to say, each can recognize that the other has a thought-out case which merits a thought-out answer. (After all, that is the sort of relationship which ought to hold between rational, civilized, individuals who confront each other on equal terms.) Even so, it must remain the case that neither can find the other's position justified in the sense of finding it *fully persuasive*. If that were to happen, then P and Q would simply swap places, with P voting for the introduction of publicly financed health care and Q voting against it. However, that is not the situation we are being asked to envisage by advocates of deliberative democracy. We are being asked to suppose that each can find the other's argument 'justified' while – at the same time – sticking to his or her own position and voting intention. This looks a lot like asking someone to believe that it is raining while, at the same time, believing that it is not raining; so there is, clearly, a question here as to whether the deliberative democrat's position is coherent.

Before moving on, I should explain that my intention in this section has only been to indicate theoretical obstacles by which an defence of the deliberative democratic idea appears to be confronted. I am sure that deliberative democrats will have answers to difficulties such as those I have outlined. Indeed, deliberative democracy is such an attractive ideal that it is to be hoped that they will. Here, it would be interesting to speculate as to what those answers might be. However, it is time to move on.

How realistic is deliberative democracy's vision of the good society?

Recall that the force-field model's aspirations to credibility are largely founded in its claim to present a realistic picture of modern society. By itself, this makes it worth considering whether the model's rival, deliberative democracy, can sustain a similar claim. Bear in mind also that deliberative democracy is, quite unashamedly, a theoretical construct, developed and refined by academics. The usual philistine accusations of ivory tower-ism are lurking in the shadows here, so we need to consider how, if at all, their threat can be resisted.

Now note that there is a twofold answer to the above question. We need to consider the extent to which society *as it is* can be described in terms of the deliberative model, but we also need to consider whether it *has the potential to develop* into a form which matches the model more closely. Here, let me simply express my own opinion that deliberative democracy's vision can appear more realistic now that it would have done sixty or so years ago, when R.A.Dahl published *A Preface to Democratic Theory*. At that time, any self-respecting teacher of political philosophy would have argued that a direct democracy such as that exemplified by the ancient Athenian assembly was, by now, an impossibility; that the populations of modern nation states are just too large to permit the face-to-face contact direct democracy requires. (The USA's population is now around 317 million. Try squeezing all those people into a football stadium, even the largest in the country.)

But things have changed since then, and – of course – the explanation lies in the rise of the internet. At least, it does if you take an optimistic view, for, on that view, you could argue that the internet has created an arena within which deliberation can take place between individuals who are not *spatially* face-to-face but who are nevertheless *virtually* so. Of course, you might equally well take a pessimistic view; for example, the view expressed by Bruce Ackermann and James Fishkin as follows:

> *Despite our present infatuation with the internet, the rising forces of technology threaten to make the consequences of civic privatism worse, not better. We have a public dialogue that is ever more efficiently segmented in its audiences and morselized in its sound bites. We have an ever more tabloid news agenda dulling the sensitivities of an increasingly inattentive citizenry. And we have mechanisms of feedback from the public, from viewer call-ins to self-selected internet polls that emphasize intense constituencies, unrepresentative of the public at large.*

These are claims which raise the question of what implications, if any, the rise of new technologies carry for our understanding of free speech. So, should one be optimistic or pessimistic? Perhaps it's too early to tell, or perhaps I should leave it to you, the reader, to judge.

▶ A note on the first amendment

In writing this chapter I have found myself concentrating, for the most part, upon the work of writers whose intellectual roots lie in the United States. Could this be more than an accident? I wonder. Perhaps it reflects the fact that free speech, as affirmed by the first amendment, has played a special role in the history of the United States – a role in the design of its democratic institutions. The USA is, after all, distinguished from many other nation states by the fact that its institutions were actually *designed*, and this over a period of a few months in 1787 when the Constitution was drawn up at the Philadelphia Convention. Any intelligent, educated US citizen will be familiar with the constitution, of course. It is, so to speak, in the national DNA, so could that explain why American writers on free speech, in particular, should have tended to focus upon its role in the democratic process, placing special emphasis upon the first amendment?

The first amendment began life as the first item listed in a Bill of Rights, introduced by James Madison in 1791. Madison reasoned that 'checks' were needed to protect individual liberty against the tendency of central power towards 'tyranny'. This is quite unlike Meiklejohn's reason for idealizing the town meeting. His description of the way consensus is achieved at the meeting bears more resemblance to Rousseau's account of how 'the general will' is (supposedly) determined at meetings of the general assembly. It is in line with his description of the Constitution as' [an agreement] that the people of the United States shall be self-governed' that the meeting as 'self-government in is simplest, most obvious form'. This is just one illustration of the omnipresent role the first amendment has come to play in American thought.

There is an obvious contrast with the UK here, for if Britain can be said to have a constitution at all, that is only because certain practices – certain ways of doing things – have developed over centuries. Relatively little is written down. But – as an extremely rough and ready generalization – let me hazard the view that British writers on free speech have tended to forefront the idea of a long struggle against authority; by independent conscience against religious censorship (Milton), by 'republican' against 'monarchical' elements (Hume), or by the forces of 'progress' against those of 'order' (Mill). Could this reflect an adversarial current which has run through British culture and which – as one might argue – can be traced back at least as far as Magna Carta in 1215?

Well, it's a thought at least, and it prompts the further speculation that it may be no accident, either, that it should have been philosophers from mainland Europe who have tended to emphasize the incremental corruption of liberal institutions from within. I mean the idea that while purportedly liberal institutions may *appear* to have remained intact, in reality they may have been deprived of their initial *raison d'être*. It was, after all, in Germany, in the earlier part of the last century, that the ultimate betrayal of the 'Enlightenment project' was experienced at first hand. One such writer is Herbert Marcuse who, in his essay 'Repressive Tolerance', argues that, for all appearances to the contrary, 'universal tolerance' in modern society has become just one more instrument of repression. Another such – also associated with the 'Frankfurt School' – is Jürgen Habermas, whose description of changes in the 'public sphere' over time we shall consider in the next chapter.

Free speech, time and change

But first, here is the opening sentence of David Hume's short essay, 'Of the Liberty of the Press'.

> *Nothing is more apt to surprise a foreigner than the extreme liberty which we enjoy in this country of communicating whatever we please and of openly censuring every measure entered into by the king or his ministers.*

Hume, the Scottish Enlightenment's leading philosopher, goes on to remark that:

> *As this liberty is not indulged in any other government, either republican or monarchical – in Holland and Venice more than in France or Spain – it may very naturally give occasion to the question: How it happens that Great Britain alone enjoys this peculiar privilege?*

Hume's essay was published in 1741, at a time when France was still an absolute monarchy and what was to become the USA no more than a motley assortment of small colonies. Bear that in mind, and it is conceivable that his description of Britain as a country which enjoyed more press freedom than anywhere else was actually correct.

So now, supposing that it was, what might the explanation have been? Well, according to Hume himself, it lay with the finely balanced separation of interests by which the British polity was characterized, with 'monarchical' and 'republican' elements continually pitted against each other. This conflict brought a particular mechanism into play, or so Hume argued. If the former element's aspirations to arbitrary power were to be held in check by the latter then, 'an easy method of conveying the alarm from one end of the kingdom to the other' was required, and, 'The spirit of the people must frequently be roused in order to curb the ambition of the court'. As Hume then argues:

> *[There is n]othing so effectual to this purpose as the liberty of the press, by which all the learning, wit, and genius of the nation may be employed on the side of freedom and everyone be animated to its defence. As long, therefore, as the republican part of our government can maintain itself against the monarchical, it will naturally be careful to keep the press open, as of importance to its own preservation.*

In short, a free press is essential if the ambitions of the powerful are to be contained.

Later in the essay, Hume reminds us that there can be variations between cultures in the degree to which they foster a climate hospitable to discussion. 'It is to be hoped', he says, 'that men, being every day more accustomed to the free discussion of public affairs, will improve in their judgement of them, and be with greater difficulty seduced by every idle rumour and popular clamour'; that is, that the liberty of the press enjoyed in Britain will foster an improved level of discussion. There is surely something right about this. At any rate, it is one thing to describe someone as 'liberal' and another to describe that person as '*a* liberal'. The former is a matter of having a certain temperament or, as it may be, of adopting an open and tolerant attitude, the latter a matter of subscribing to certain moral and political principles. Even so, it is certainly arguable that the exercise of liberal freedoms, such as free speech and the liberty of discussion, will only flourish in a culture where liberal attitudes are prevalent.

For our purposes, however, the most interesting features of Hume's argument lie in what he *doesn't* say. Note that:

1 Hume is taking the primacy of a certain technology – printing – for granted. For him, 'the liberty of the press' is, thus the liberty of printed media to be as critical of the 'monarchical' establishment as they like. (By the time he was writing, newspapers had been in existence for at least half a century. Hume also mentions 'the book' and 'the pamphlet'.)

2 He is also assuming the existence of a specific public, or audience, to whose members the publications contained in the press are addressed; a public which is literate enough to comprehend the contents of those publications. This involves assuming that literacy is distributed throughout the population in a certain way. For Hume, the readers who count are those who hold 'republican' sympathies and who are, in some cases, likely to act upon them.

Something Hume actually does mention needs to be added to the foregoing list here, and that is the fact that, as he sees it,

3 British society is divided into 'monarchical' and 'republican' elements.

My point is that, taken together, (1), (2), and (3) determine *the context* from which, according to Hume, the activities of a free press derive their justification. It follows that, should there be a change in any of one these factors, either in its nature or in its relationship to the others – or should any of them become absent altogether – then the liberty of the press might cease to have the *raison d'être* Hume says it has, that of holding the 'monarchical' powerful in check.

In emphasizing the point, I am – I suppose – reflecting the philosophical truism that action is more than mere movement. Extend your right arm horizontally, for example, and you will only be 'signalling to turn right' if you are (i) driving a car or some other road vehicle and if (ii) certain laws and conventions – 'rules of the road' – are in place. Change the context and you might be 'giving someone directions' or, at a bus stop, 'letting the driver know that you want the bus to stop and pick you up'. Deprive the movement of any context and you will only be 'extending your right arm horizontally'. Similarly, 'publishing an article in a pamphlet or newspaper' only qualifies as 'holding the powerful in check' when factors such as those listed above are in place. If it is to qualify as 'contributing to the liberty of thought and discussion' or 'making an essential contribution to the democratic decision-making process', changes in context may be required. Lock yourself in the bathroom and read passages from your favourite political manifesto – out loud, but unheard – and you are doing none of these things.

So why didn't Hume state his assumptions, (1) and (2) in explicit terms? The most likely explanation is that it would never have occurred to him to do so. But even if it had, he would probably have considered it ridiculously pedantic to go to the trouble. This was the eighteenth century after all, and *how else* would ideas have been disseminated if not through the printed word? For our purposes, however, it is far from pedantic to take note of these assumptions, the reason being that they refer to *variables*; that is, to factors whose nature can change over time. You will see what I mean if you compare the situation assumed by Hume with the following.

> *1859: (This is the year in which Mill's* On Liberty *is published.) Literacy – the ability to read – has increased since Milton's time and it is, by now, nearly universal. There is a new and rising, aspirational upper working/lower middle class. The latter is conformist and likes to think of itself as 'respectable'. (It is the 'majority' of whose 'tyranny' Mill was so fearful.) With these developments there has been a corresponding increase in the degree of heterogeneity by which the reading public is marked. Within it, it is now possible to discern 'popular' and 'highbrow' elements. On the one hand, there are readers of popular newspapers and there is an appetite for the work of novelists such as Dickens. On the other, intellectuals are catered for by 'heavy' journals to which individuals such as Mill himself contribute –* The Westminster Review, The London Review, *and* The Examiner, *for example. (These were, I suppose, nineteenth century equivalents of the* London *or* New York Review of Books.) Of course,*

the boundaries between the two reading 'publics' was by no means rigid, and many people would have fallen into both categories.

2015 (i.e. now)*: The printed word is fast ceasing to be the primary medium of communication. Perhaps it has already ceased to be that. Media take diverse forms. We live in the age of the internet. Instantaneous communication from any point in the world to any other point is now a reality. Mass surveillance of the public by the state is possible, and, so far as anyone can ascertain, actually takes place.*

As I pointed out in chapter two, Mill welcomed the increase in literacy and the accompanying eagerness to engage in discussion by which his age was marked. 'Men may not reason better, concerning the great questions in which human nature is interested, but they reason more' he remarked, 'and if no greater numbers than before have attained the higher degrees of intelligence, fewer grovel in that state of abject stupidity, which can only co-exist with utter apathy and sluggishness.' But if the generality of the population ('men') were not reasoning 'better' we have, on the face of things, no reason to suppose that *they* were pitting ideas against each other in a manner, sophisticated enough to facilitate the pursuit of truth. However, it is the gist of his argument for 'the liberty of thought and discussion' that *some* people are capable of doing just that. So, my point is that Mill's argument could only have gained a purchase on reality if my sketch of the world in 1859, above, is roughly accurate.

▶ Whatever happened to the public sphere?

My subject in this chapter, then, is the relation between theoretical accounts of free speech such as those I have been discussing throughout this book and the reality they are intended to illuminate. My discussion of Hume in the previous section suggests that the relationship may turn out to be complex for, just as there can be considerable variation between theories, so reality can change over time. At any rate, this is true of social, technological and political reality – that is, the reality to which the theories in question mainly relate – and it means that we are, in a sense, aiming at a moving target. Of course, it would be ridiculous to criticize Milton or Hume for having failed to foresee the technological changes by which the centuries subsequent to their own would be characterized, but we have the benefit of hindsight and should be more circumspect. To put it another way, now – in the twenty-first century – there may be little point in defending free speech *as if* one were still living in the eighteenth.

However, rather than criticize this or that writer for having paid too little attention to context let me turn instead to a philosopher who is exceptional for having paid a great deal of attention to it, namely Jürgen Habermas. Here, I am thinking especially of his early work, *The Structural Transformation of the Public Sphere*, the central theme of which is the development and subsequent 'transformation' of a 'public sphere'.

According to Habermas, this came to full fruition in Europe, and in the period which stretched from the middle years of the seventeenth century to the late eighteenth.

▲ A coffee house, London eighteenth century

Let me quote him at some length. The following passage, in which Habermas describes the 'coffee-house' culture which developed during that period, will give a flavour of what he has in mind.

> The predominance of the 'town' was strengthened by new institutions that, for all their variety, in Great Britain and France took over the same social functions; the coffee houses in their golden age between 1680 and 1730 and the salons in the period between regency and revolution. In both countries they were centres of criticism – literary at first, then

also political – in which began to emerge, between aristocratic society and bourgeois intellectuals, a certain parity of the educated.

Around the middle of the seventeenth century after not only tea – first to be popular – but also chocolate and coffee had become the common beverages of at least the well-to-do strata of the population, the coachman of a Levantine merchant opened the first coffee house. By the first decade of the eighteenth century London already had 3,000 of them, each with a group of regulars. Just as Dryden, surrounded by the new generation of writers, joined the battle of the 'ancients and moderns' at Will's. Addison and Steele a little later convened their 'little senate' at Button's; so too in the Rotary Club, presided over by Milton's secretary, Marvell and Pepys met with Harrington who here probably presented the republican ideas of his Oceana.

In 1715, not long after the beginning of the eighteenth century, London's population numbered around 630,000, so, if Habermas's figure of 3,000 coffee houses in 1700 is correct, that works out at one coffee house per 210 Londoners. That's a lot of coffee houses, especially when one considers that a sizeable proportion of the population would have been quite uninterested in intellectual matters. Middle class, literate London must indeed have been a vibrant place.

But for our purposes the most salient features of the coffee-house culture, as described by Habermas were as follows: First, there is the fact that, inside the coffee houses, discussion was unsupervised and uncontrolled by authority. People were free to discuss what they liked, with the result that the coffee-houses were regarded by the authorities as seedbeds of political unrest. (Habermas cites a proclamation of the early 1670s which declared that, 'Men have assumed to themselves a liberty, not only in coffee-houses, but in other places and meetings, both public and private, to censure and defame the proceedings of the State, by speaking evil of things they understand not, and endeavouring to create and nourish an universal jealousie and dissatisfaction in the minds of all His Majesties good subjects'.) Second, there is the fact that the public sphere was an arena within which people confronted each other as equals. *Anyone* could join in. Of course, the people who were *in fact* educated to a level which rendered them capable of joining in were middle class – which is no doubt one reason why Habermas sometimes refers to the 'bourgeois' public sphere – but, in *ethos*, it was essentially classless.

Of course, the phenomenon Habermas describes was not confined to London. He is merely using the history of London as a case study. Nor was the institution of the coffee-house the public sphere's only constituent. As noted, he also mentions the French literary *salon*. Moreover, this was a time when the first newspapers were coming into existence, and which saw the rise to prominence of a new profession, the political journalist. (Says Habermas, 'Men like Pope, Gay, Arbuthnot, and Swift combined literature and politics in a peculiar fashion comparable to Addison's and Steele's combination of literature and journalism'.) So, *this* was the world into which Hume was to introduce his essay on the liberty of the press.

What of the modern world? To be more precise, what of the world in 1962, the year in which *The Structural Transformation of the Public Sphere* was first published? Well, compare Habermas's description of eighteenth century coffee-house culture with the following passage, in which he describes the 'managed' – or should that be 'tamed'? – form which, as he sees it, debate and discussion so typically assume when presented by contemporary media.

> *radio stations, publishers and associations have turned the staging of panel discussions into a flourishing secondary business. Thus, discussion seems to be carefully cultivated and there seems to be no barrier to its proliferation. But surreptitiously it has changed in a specific way: it assumes the form of a consumer item. ... Today the conversation itself is administered. Professional dialogues from the podium, panel discussions, and round table shows – the rational debate of private people become one of the production of the stars in radio and television, a saleable package ready for the box office; it assumes commodity form even at 'conferences' where anyone can 'participate'. Discussion, now a 'business' becomes formalised; the presentation of positions and counter positions is bound to certain prearranged rules of the game; consensus about the subject matter is made largely superfluous by that concerning form.*

Or, take the following description of the manner in which the popular press now operates.

> *By means of variegated type and layout and ample illustration reading is made easy at the same time that its field of spontaneity in general is restricted by serving up the material as a ready-made convenience, patterned and pre-digested. ... In addition, the share of political or politically relevant news changes. Public affairs, social problems, economic matters, education and health – according to a categorisation suggest by American authors, precisely the 'delayed reward news' – are not only pushed into the background by 'immediate reward news' (comics, corruption, accidents, disasters, sports, recreation, social events, and human interest) but, as the characteristic label already indicates, are also actually read less and more rarely.*

How accurate are these descriptions? In my opinion, the former description of 'managed conversation' is all too redolent of the type of TV programme in which 'discussion' is predetermined by the fact that a panel of four or five individuals has been selected, each for his or her known political affiliation, be it Left, Right, or intermediate. Usually, the ensuing 'discussion' consists of little more than a serial reiteration of rehearsed party lines. Or consider the orchestrated TV debates between party leaders which have become commonplace in the US and the UK at election times. Suitably groomed, the candidates hope to do no more than pronounce the catchy lines with which they have been primed, and the 'winner' is deemed to be the person whose performance has most immediately impressed the viewing audience; that is, not the candidate whose argument deserves to be judged the best when measured with reference to more objective standards of rationality and evidence. Likewise, in the second passage, it seems to me that Habermas gives quite a good description of the way the contemporary tabloid press operates.

But against this, could it be that I'm being a little too cynical and pessimistic? Certainly, one commentator, James Gordon Finlayson, has described Habermas's 'account of the way the culture industry created an increasingly homogeneous mass of docile and uncritical consumers' as 'rather grim'. Then again, there may be reasons for optimism which could not have been foreseen in 1962. For example, there is the fact that, 'video cameras, satellite as well as mobile phones, voice recorders and document scanners, combined with the technical ease of uploading their output to the world wide web, create new possibilities for recording, sharing and debating current history – not to mention archiving it for posterity' (so observed Timothy Garton Ash, writing in 2012.) Then again, it is now possible for ordinary people with mobile phones to film and disseminate images of repression, violence and atrocity, simply by recording it and posting the video on the internet for all to see.

Still, for our purposes the *precise* accuracy of Habermas's account is beside the point. It only matters that it should be accurate *enough*, and it is pretty clear that the two worlds he distinguishes – the eighteenth century 'coffee-house' world and our own – are different, and in respects similar to those he describes. (As I remarked in my discussion of deliberative democracy, it is quite often easier to say what a thing is not than to say what it is. To put it another way, while the Earth is not a perfect sphere, and while no-one is quite sure just what shape it is, it is certainly not a cube and certainly not flat.) Similar considerations apply to his account of how the public sphere of the earlier period became subverted and transformed into the media-permeated environment of the twentieth century. Habermas's own account – which is subtle and detailed – reflects the thinking of the 'Frankfurt School' with which he was associated. Fundamental processes – economic and social – are represented as culminating in the subversion of Enlightenment principles, while at the same time maintaining the illusion that those principles are respected. In this short chapter, it would be impossible to explain, let alone evaluate, Habermas's story. But, in any case, for our purposes the point is only that *there is a story to be told here*, and one to be borne in mind when evaluating claims which invoke the value of free speech.

By way of example, take the claim I referred to a moment ago; that it is the function of the press to 'speak truth to power'. Now, if we are to believe Habermas – and, likewise, Hume – in the eighteenth century speaking truth to power was one of the press's main functions, perhaps its only major function. At any rate, that is what I take to be the burden of Hume's argument that if 'the republican part of our government [is to] maintain itself against the monarchical, it will naturally be careful to keep the press open'. But now, while it may remain true that the press speaks truth to power, there is a great deal else it does as well – and that can include the pretty nasty demonisation of minority groups. Take the case of German Jews, who, 'had been fellow citizens before 1933' but, by the time Germany invaded Poland in 1939 [they] no longer belonged to Germans' universe of moral obligation' So writes the historian Claudia Koonz in her study, *The Nazi Conscience* and, as she adds, 'This transformation did not just happen. The expulsion of Jews from Germans' universe of moral obligation was carefully engineered'.

Koonz goes on to document, in detail, how the latter transformation was engineered, and it is clear that the German popular press, through the use of cartoons, propaganda and so on, had a considerable role to play. It would be hard to describe this as a simple case of speaking truth to power. It has far more in common with the promulgation of 'hate speech' and of course – it almost goes without saying – the press has not learnt to behave any better – either in Germany or anywhere else.

Habermas: a conclusion and an observation

The conclusion I draw here is, in fact, the one I have been emphasizing all along in this chapter. It is that, if you are writing in the twenty-first century there is no point in pretending that you are still living in the eighteenth. Thus, if you want to advocate a 'free' press – that is, a press which is not subject to legislative control – an argument such as Hume's, that the press holds power to account by confronting it with truth, will only serve your purposes to the extent that there are sections of the press which do just that. It won't help you defend other press activities such as the demonisation of vulnerable minority groups or, for that matter, tapping peoples' mobile phones and recording their private conversations with a view to satisfying a public appetite for salacious gossip. If you really want to defend *those* activities, you will have to think of a different argument.

As for the observation, it is that, Habermas's description of an early modern 'public sphere' exemplifies a *motif* which has recurred throughout my discussion in this book, for, with it, he is idealizing a situation in which rationally disposed individuals confront each other as equals and enter into discussion and argument. More than anything else, it is the recurrence of this idea throughout the literature which has impressed me as I have been writing, and I shall return to it in a moment.

▶ In conclusion

With that, it's time to bring this book to a close. To that end, let me now list some of the points to which I have, perhaps, been giving insufficient emphasis. No doubt there are quite a few, but I shall stick to the following.

First: I have been assuming throughout that more speech is better than less – in other words that a world in which people are free to perform a wide variety of 'speech acts', and in which they actually exercise that freedom, is better than one in which they are not and do not. (Of course, I am including acts which do not literally involve speech here. See my discussion of Picasso's *Guernica* in chapter one.) If anything justifies this assumption, it is the fact that it is our capacity for language which distinguishes us most sharply from other animals. At any rate, so I am inclined to think. In other words, we are talkative animals. More than that, the way we socialize, organize our institutions, think, create – neither these nor any other human activity would be possible without language. Language helps structure our very existence, so how could there *not* be a moral presupposition in favour of our being free to use it?

Problems arise because – of course – other things are not always equal. Sometimes there may be good reasons for supressing freedom of speech, so we need to determine what acts ought to be protected, even when those reasons apply. (See my discussion of the differences between *OK* magazine's feature on Cindy Crawford and the 'Snowden revelations' – also in chapter one.) It should be clear that each of the theories I have been discussing draws a different line between those speech acts which, as it claims, merit special protection and those which do not. To avoid misunderstanding, perhaps I should add that they are by no means mutually exclusive. In other words, it doesn't follow that if some version of the argument from truth, say, were to turn out to be correct, other arguments – arguments from deliberative democracy, for example – would be automatically invalidated. Moreover, a speech act which failed to qualify for protection on the grounds set out by John Stuart Mill might still qualify on the grounds articulated by Meiklejohn or Dahl. Again, wouldn't it be surprising if there were *only one* argument for free speech, given the diversity of the roles played by language in our day-to-day life?

Now let me turn, secondly, to the conception of a realm, or 'sphere' within which rationally disposed individuals confront each other as equals with a view to engaging in discussion. We first encountered this idea with my introduction of a 'discussion group model' in chapter one. It was the model I used to supply a context with which to make sense claims such as 'there is no such thing as the right not to be offended'. We encountered it again in the assumptions underpinning Mill's defence of the liberty of thought and discussion – and yet again in arguments for 'deliberative democracy'. Again, it figures in Habermas's account of a 'public sphere' which has become corrupted over time. As I remarked a moment ago, it is a motif which has run, over time, throughout the literature on free speech. As I have been suggesting, this conception represents an ideal to which actual societies may strive to correspond; that, when viewed from the perspective of liberalism, the more a society resembles the ideal, the more there is to recommend it.

The probability of my being misunderstood on this point is so high that I must, of necessity, emphasize the following. For a start, I am *not* suggesting that society at large should be made to resemble some vast seminar room within whose walls 'discussion' is confined to a decorous conversation between grey bearded professors. How depressingly stuffy that would be! What would happen to art, to literature, or – for that matter – to *OK* magazine? But I am suggesting no such thing, and you could only conclude that I am by ignoring my insistence that any credible argument for free speech must count a wide variety of acts as contributions to the 'discussion'. Works of art, musical performances, political cartoons, much else besides must also count – and not just verbal contributions to some formalized debate. Again, I am *not* engaged in the revisionist exercise of restricting the speech acts people ought to be free to perform to a relatively limited category. To accuse me of that would be to ignore the point upon which I have just been insisting, namely that there is a moral presupposition in favour of peoples' being free to perform all manner of speech acts. To make that general presupposition, and to add that the freedom to speak should be restricted, only when there are very good reasons for doing so, is to leave a great deal of space for the exercise of that freedom. It doesn't look like revisionism to me.

Other models are available, of course – patterns to which, according to some, it is desirable that society should conform. These include various versions of the idea that institutions should be shaped, and individuals organized, in accordance with the demands of this, that, or the other ideology; that is, in accordance with the demands of God, or history, or whatever. Such ideas have not always proven popular, and certainly not with those who have found themselves having to be coerced into complying with the ideology's demands, or even being killed in its name. More than that – and more to the point here – if you coerce someone into complying with beliefs to which he or she does not actually subscribe, you treat that person neither as an equal nor as an adult. By contrast with that type of pattern – which I suppose we should call 'totalitarian' – the idea of a public sphere or arena postulates a situation in which individuals confront each other as both, owing each other equal respect. This is preferable, or so I would argue, but not only because equality is good in itself (the latter being a claim with which you may or may not agree). It is because we do *in fact* inhabit a world in which we are, perforce, constrained to share the planet with others whose ideas and aspirations we do not share, and in which confronting those others with equal respect is the only realistic alternative. (By contrast, in pre-Reformation Europe, it might have seemed realistic to suppose that society should be organized hierarchically, in accordance with the demands of some all-embracing religious vision. It can't be deemed realistic now. One great virtue of the 'public sphere' idea, then, is that it reflects contemporary reality in a way others do not.)

Thirdly, and finally, let me state the following opinion: One frequently hears it remarked that 1989, the year in which the Berlin wall was demolished, represented a watershed in Western history. I agree that 1989 was significant but, if I were asked, I would say that the most significant moment in European history came in 1945, when fascism was eradicated and centralised authoritarianism beaten into retreat, forced back behind the 'iron curtain' in the east and, in the west, south of the Pyrenees. (Historians might argue that the demise of Franco in 1975, and then the collapse of the wall in 1989, represent the end-point of the latter process.)

Since then, we have enjoyed a period of relative calm and, as a result, it has become far too easy to be complacent. There is no telling when those sinister scarecrows might return to haunt us, emerging from the subterranean caverns to which they were exiled.

And then, isn't it rather ironic that this book should form part of a series entitled 'all that matters'? In fact, no single book on free speech could include all that matters on the subject. I don't just mean that for all the effort I have put into developing the theoretical arguments which have formed the subject of these chapters, there remains empirical work which only you, the reader, can do, although that may be true enough. For example, even if you agree with me that 'hate speech' is a different thing from, say, the pursuit of truth through thought and discussion – and that the two should be treated in different ways – you may still have to decide, in a certain case, whether it falls into one category or the other or, indeed, whether it falls into both or even many. (This is, perhaps, an area which is especially complicated by the fact that the subject of evaluation can fall into several categories. The notorious 'Danish Cartoons' may be a case in point. Again, it can happen that a 'red-top' paper which normally carries frivolous material, and which is occasionally open to accusations of prejudice against minorities, will sometimes publish serious journalism too. How does one deal with such cases? Well, there is no 'automatic answer', which can decide the point one way or the other. You have to shift for yourself.)

Moreover, there is the fact that it is up to you, the reader, to decide for yourself what to make of my arguments. After all, this is philosophy – an activity which thrives upon disagreement and intellectual discord. Still, the point is not to describe 'all that matters' so much as to ensure that the arguments for free speech are continually subjected to critical review. It is the only way to ensure that the idea of free speech itself is kept alive and protected from the fate John Stuart Mill described so eloquently, that of degenerating into dogma, 'the meaning of the doctrine itself ... in danger of being lost or enfeebled, and deprived of its vital effect on the character and conduct; the dogma becoming a mere formal profession, inefficacious for good, but cumbering the ground and preventing the growth of any real and heartfelt conviction from reason or personal experience'. Free speech is far too important for that.

▲ 'Speakers' Corner, London: A Suffragette Rally

This 100 Ideas section gives ways you can explore the subject in more depth. It's much more than just the usual reading list.

5 famous documents (on the subject of free speech)

1   [T]he Freedome of Speech and Debates or Proceedings in Parlyament ought not to be impeached or questioned in any Court or Place out of Parlyament.

    (*Bill of Rights*, England, 1688)

2   Congress shall make no law respecting an establishment of religion, or prohibiting the free exercise thereof; or abridging the freedom of speech, or of the press; or of the right of the people peaceably to assemble, and to petition the government for a redress of grievances.

    (*United States Constitution*, 1787: First Amendment)

3   No one shall be disquieted on account of his opinions, including his religious views, provided their manifestation does not disturb the public order established by law.

The free communication of ideas and opinions is one of the most precious of the rights of man. Every citizen may, accordingly, speak, write, and print with freedom, but shall be responsible for such abuses of this freedom as shall be defined by law.

(*Declaration of the Rights of Man and Citizen*, France, 1789: Articles 10 & 11.)

4 Everyone has the right to freedom of thought, conscience and religion; this right includes freedom to change his religion or belief, and freedom, either alone or in community with others and in public or private, to manifest his religion or belief in teaching, practice, worship and observance.

Everyone has the right to freedom of opinion and expression; this right includes freedom to hold opinions without interference and to seek, receive and impart information and ideas through any media and regardless of frontiers.

(*Universal Declaration of Human Rights*, United Nations, 1948, Articles 18 & 19)

5 Everyone has the right to freedom of expression. This right shall include freedom to hold opinions and to receive and impart information and ideas without interference by public authority and regardless of frontiers. This Article shall not prevent States from requiring the licensing of broadcasting, television or cinema enterprises.

(*European Convention on Human Rights*, 1953: Article 10)

15 books

The list includes philosophical 'classics' and some recent treatments of free speech

6 John Milton (1644), *Areopagitica.*

7 John Locke (1689), *A Letter Concerning Toleration*: A famous defence of religious toleration.

8 John Locke (1690), *Second Treatise of Civil Government*: Locke's argument for limited government starts out from the premise that everyone possess 'inalienable' natural rights to life, liberty and property. The *Second Treatise* is a foundational liberalism document. There is no direct treatment of free speech, but Locke's influence is obvious in – for example – the wording of the US Constitution.

9 Edmund Burke (1790), *Reflections on the Revolution in France*: A sceptical critique of the ideals which informed the revolution, including the idea that there are rights, as listed in the *Declaration of the Rights of Man and Citizen*. (see above)

10 John Stuart Mill (1859), *On Liberty*: The second chapter contains Mill's influential defence of 'the liberty of thought and discussion'.

11 James Fitzjames Stephen (1874), *Liberty, Equality, Fraternity*: An early critique of Mill's argument.

12 Karl Marx & Friedrich Engels (1888), *The Communist Manifesto*: Marx and Engels state that, 'Law, morality, religion, are to him [the proletarian] so many bourgeois prejudices, behind which lurk in ambush just as many bourgeois interests'. How would this stricture apply to the idea that there is a right to free speech?

13 J.B. Bury (1914), *A History of Freedom of Thought*: Humanity is portrayed as steadily moving along the road from superstitious darkness to rationalistic light. Some would call this an Enlightenment fantasy. To be read with caution.

14 Jürgen Habermas (1962), *The Structural Transformation of the Public Sphere*.

15 Isaiah Berlin (1969), *Four Essays on Liberty*: Contains his seminal essay, 'Two Concepts of Liberty'. Berlin was one of liberalism's most eloquent, and most interesting, advocates.

16 John Rawls (1971): *A Theory of Justice*: In this imaginative work, Rawls constructs a 'social contract' defence of liberal values. Rawls is widely considered to have been the late twentieth century's most significant political philosopher.

17 John Rawls (1993), *Political Liberalism*: Rawls endeavours to solve 'the problem of political liberalism', i.e., 'How is it possible for there to exist over time a just and stable society of free and equal citizens, who remain profoundly divided by reasonable religious, philosophical, and moral doctrines.'

18 Stanley Fish (1994): *There's No Such Thing as Free Speech: And a Good Thing Too*.

19 Alan Haworth (1998): *Free Speech*.

20 Nigel Warburton (2009): *Free Speech: A Very Short Introduction*.

5 more constitutions

Two more constitutions which emphasize the right to free speech

21 *Constitution of the Peoples' Republic of China*, Article 35: Citizens of the People's Republic of China enjoy freedom of speech, of the press, of assembly, of association, of procession and of demonstration.

(Question: How consistent is this with the constitution's article 1, which states that, 'The People's Republic of China is a socialist state under the people's democratic dictatorship led by the working class and based on the alliance of workers and peasants', and that, 'The socialist system is the basic system of the People's Republic of China. Disruption of the socialist system by any organization or individual is prohibited'?)

22 *Socialist Constitution of the Democratic People's Republic of [North] Korea*, Article 67: Citizens are guaranteed freedom of speech, the press, assembly, demonstration and association.

(Question: How consistent is this with the constitution's article 2, which states, 'The Democratic People's Republic of Korea is a revolutionary State which has inherited the brilliant traditions formed during the glorious revolutionary struggle against the imperialist aggressors and in the struggle to achieve the liberation of the homeland and the freedom and well-being of the people'?)

Three constitutions which place limits on the right to free speech.

23 *Saudi Arabia, Constitution*, Article 39 (Expression): Information, publication, and all other media shall employ courteous language and the state's regulations, and they shall contribute to the education of the nation and the bolstering of its unity. All acts that foster sedition or division or harm the state's security and its public relations or detract from man's dignity and rights shall be prohibited. The statutes shall define all that.

24 *Constitution of the Republic of Cuba*, 1992, Article 53: Citizens have freedom of speech and of the press in keeping with the objectives of socialist society. Material conditions for the exercise of that right are provided by the fact that the press, radio, television, cinema, and other mass media are state or social property and can never be private property. This assures their use at exclusive service of the working people and in the interests of society.

25 *Constitution of the Islamic Republic of Iran*, Article 24: Publications and the press have freedom of expression except when it is detrimental to the fundamental principles of Islam or the rights of the public. The details of this exception will be specified by law.

9 landmark court cases

26 The trial of Socrates (Athens, 399BC): Socrates was convicted on the trumped-up charges of corrupting the city's youth and disrespecting its gods. He was sentenced to death. Socrates is frequently portrayed as a martyr for freedom of thought, although some authorities argue that his real 'crime' was to sympathise with Sparta, against whom Athens had been bitterly at war for over three decades.

27 John Wilkes: Wilkes was a radical journalist and politician. He ran into trouble with the authorities on a number of occasions, once for attacking a speech by King George 3rd and, another time, for writing a poem considered both pornographic and subversive. In 1764, he was tried *in absentia* and declared an outlaw. He was eventually imprisoned in 1768. 'Wilkes and Liberty!' became a popular cry.

28 Schenck v. United States (1914): The landmark case in which Justice Wendell Holmes stated his 'clear and present danger' doctrine. (See chapter 1, p.12 ff.)

29 State of Tennessee v. John Thomas Scopes, 1925, otherwise known as 'the Monkey Trial'. Scopes, a high school teacher, was accused of violating Tennessee's Butler Act. This made it illegal to teach human evolution in any state-funded school. Scopes was found guilty but, later, acquitted on a technicality. The trial was instrumental in bringing attention to the conflict between up-to-date scientific theory and religious fundamentalism in the US.

30 'The Lady Chatterley Trial' (Regina v. Penguin Books Ltd.), 1960: Penguin, who had published the unexpurgated version of D.H. Lawrence's *Lady Chatterley's Lover*, had been charged with violating the Obscene Publications Act. The jury found for the defence. Could this have been the start of 'the swinging sixties'?

31 The Oz trial, 1971: *Oz*, described as a 'satirical magazine' was closely associated with the 'counter-culture' (free love, psychedelic drugs, etc.) Issue 28, 'the schoolkids' issue' created quite a scandal. It contained anti-authoritarian contributions from teenage school students, and drawings of Rupert Bear, the children's character, in sexually explicit positions. The three editors were sentenced to prison, but the verdict was overturned on appeal.

32 USA v. Progressive, Inc (1979): Howard Morland was a journalist who figured out how to build a hydrogen bomb. The design was then a state secret, but Morland relied entirely upon publicly available sources. He proposed to publish the results of his research in *The Progressive*, a radical magazine. Unsurprisingly, the authorities became worried and a court case ensued. Morland invoked the First Amendment, the case was dropped, and the article eventually published. Interestingly, no-one has yet been blown up as a consequence.

33 R. v. Keegstra (Canada, 1990): James Keegstra was a schoolteacher and he was also an enthusiastic Holocaust denier. Whilst in class, he would make his antisemitic opinions perfectly apparent. The Supreme Court of Canada judged that Keegstra had violated the Criminal Code of Canada provision prohibiting the wilful promotion of hatred against an identifiable group as constitutional, thereby overruling Keegstra's defence that he was merely exercising a right to freedom of expression.

34 The Irving libel case (1996): David Irving sued Deborah Lipstadt for libel for having called him a Holocaust denier. Irving lost the case. (See chapter 2, p.48 ff.)

11 locations

Locations associated with the exercise of free speech.

35 The Areopagus, Athens: In ancient times, the Council of Elders met upon this rock. Saint Paul preached a famous sermon from it. The title of Milton's *Areopagitica* is a reference to it.

36 The Pnyx: Also in Athens, its where the Assembly held its meetings.

37 Independence Hall, Philadelphia: The US Constitution was signed there in 1787.

38 Speakers' Corner, Hyde Park, London: Anyone can turn up there and address the assembled crowd (should there be one).

39 The Lincoln Memorial, Washington DC: It's where Martin Luther King delivered his 'I Have a Dream' speech on August 28 1963.

Locations associated with the suppression of freedom of speech and thought

40 Bibliotecha Alexandrina, Alexandria, Egypt: Described as a 'landmark contemporary library complex', it is the successor of an earlier 'great library', reputedly the brainchild of Alexander the Great and said to contain 'all the knowledge in the world'. This is said to have been razed to the ground by fire when Egypt was conquered by the Arabs in 640AD. According to one legend, this was done on the instructions of the Caliph, who reasoned as follows: 'These books will either contradict the Koran, in which case they are heresy, or they will agree with it, in which case they are superfluous'.

41 Castillo San Jorge, Seville, Spain – once the Spanish Inquisition's HQ and now a museum: The Inquisition – established in 1480 – would torture heretics, Jews, and anyone else who held the 'wrong' beliefs. The idea was that, by getting them to renounce their beliefs, you would save their souls. That was the Inquisition's story anyway.

42 Tiananmen Square, Beijing, China: In June 1989, the square was the scene of massive demonstrations calling for government accountability, freedom of the press, freedom of speech, and the restoration of workers' control over industry. The demonstration was put down by the authorities, using military force.

43 The Opernplatz, Berlin: In May 1933, it was the site of a public book burning by groups of Nazi zealots. 25,000 books, including works by Brecht, Einstein, Marx, Hemingway and H.G.Wells were incinerated for being Jewish, 'un-German, or otherwise 'degenerate'.

44 The STASI museum, Berlin, Germany: The STASI was the East German security service – i.e. the secret police. It monitored the activities of private citizens through the use of, e.g. microphones concealed in their houses, secretly reading their mail, a collection of elaborate disguises, and with the help of a tightly controlled network of citizen informants. (These days they would just have to monitor your emails.) Other STASI museums are in Leipzig, Dresden, and Rostock

45 6, Rue Nicolas Appert, Paris, scene of the *Charlie Hebdo* massacre.

10 one-liners (other than, 'I disagree with what you say, but I will defend to the death your right to say it' – as Voltaire didn't say.)

The following lines from John Stuart Mill's *On Liberty* are much quoted.

46 If all mankind minus one were of one opinion, mankind would be no more justified in silencing that one person than he, if he had the power, would be justified in silencing mankind.

47 All silencing of discussion is an assumption of infallibility.

Here are some other good ones.

48 Everyone is in favour of free speech. Hardly a day passes without its being extolled, but some people's idea of it is that they are free to say what they like, but if anyone else says anything back, that is an outrage. (Winston Churchill)

49 All tyranny needs to gain a foothold is for people of good conscience to remain silent. (Edmund Burke)

50 Without freedom of speech we might be in the swamp. (Bob Dylan, *Motorpsycho Nightmare*)

51 I only used to drink tea out of the mug. (Mathews Ntshiwa, on being sentenced to eighteen months in prison for drinking from a mug bearing the words *Free Nelson Mandela*)

52 Freedom is the freedom to say that two plus two make four. If that is granted, all else follows. (George Orwell)

53 Freedom of Speech, that's some motherf**kin' bullshit; You say the wrong thing, they'll lock your ass up quick; The FCC says "Profanity - No Airplay"?; They can s**k my d**k while I take a s**t all day. (Ice T, *Freedom of Speech*: Ice T sounds a sceptical note. He may have a point. I felt I had to insert asterisks here...)

Finally, two ironic 'takes' on examples discussed in this book.

54 I may not agree with you, but I will defend to the death your right to make an ass of yourself. (Oscar Wilde)

55 Free speech is the right to shout 'Theatre!' in a crowded fire. (Abbie Hoffman, co-founder of the Youth International Party – aka 'Yippies')

5 items of art/artwork

56 Eugène Delacroix, *Liberty Leading the People*, in the Louvre, Paris

57 Norman Rockwell, Freedom of Speech; postage stamp featuring the famous painting. See, for example, https://www.pinterest.com/popattym/us-postage-stamps/

58 *Free Speech*, -graffiti: http://www.frontlin.es/free-speech-fukt-street-art/

59 Banksy *If graffiti changed anything it would be illegal* – graffiti http://www.unurth.com/Banksy-If-Graffiti-Changed-Anything-London

60 Free speech monument Berkeley, California: see, http://www.ucira.ucsb.edu/berkeleys-invisible-monument-to-free-speech/

5 things people do on the internet

Where, if at all, does the right to free speech enter the picture?

61 Blogging: Everyone his or her own columnist.

62 Trolling: 'the anti-social act of causing of interpersonal conflict and shock-value controversy online' – can involve hate-speech, bullying, and worse.

63 Entering a 'chat room': Public sphere or private cubicle?

64 Keeping your Facebook page up to date: A nice idea, but can be closely monitored.

65 'Tweeting': Can you really say anything intelligent with just 140 characters?

3 famous definitions of 'freedom

66 LIBERTY, or freedom, signifieth properly the absence of opposition (by opposition, I mean external impediments of motion); and may be applied no less to irrational and inanimate creatures than to rational. For whatsoever is so tied, or environed, as it cannot move but within a certain space, which space is determined by the opposition of some external body, we say it hath not liberty to go further. And so of all living creatures, whilst they are imprisoned, or restrained with walls or chains; and of the water whilst it is kept in by banks or vessels that otherwise would spread itself into a larger space; we use to say they are not at liberty to move in such manner as without those external impediments they would. (Thomas Hobbes, *Leviathan*, 1651)

67 Freedom is obedience to a law one prescribes to oneself. (Jean Jacques Rousseau, *The Social Contract*, 1762)

68 'Freedom' is just another word for nothing left to lose: Kris Kristofferson

3 famous one-liners on the subject of liberty

69 They who can give up essential liberty to obtain a little temporary safety deserve neither liberty nor safety.: Benjamin Franklin

70 It is true that liberty is precious – so precious that it must be carefully rationed: V.I. Lenin

71 Freedom for the pike is death for the minnows: Isaiah Berlin

1 play and 9 movies

72 *The Crucible* (1953): Arthur Miller's play is a dramatisation of the witch trials which were conducted in Salem Massachusetts in 1692-3. However, his real target is Jo McCarthy's campaign against 'un-American activities'.

73 *Inherit the Wind* (1960): Director Stanley Kramer's subject is the Scopes 'Monkey Trial'. Spencer Tracy stars as a lawyer for the defence, Gene Kelly as a reporter, and Dick York as the teacher Bertram Cates.

74 *Fahrenheit 451* (1966): Directed by Francois Truffaut and based on the novel by Ray Bradbury, a science-fiction movie set in a future where all books and reading materials are banned. Stars Julie Christie and Oskar Werner.

75 *All the President's Men* (1976): Intrepid reporters Bob Woodward and Carl Bernstein (Robert Redford and Dustin Hoffman) doggedly pursue the truth about Nixon's misdemeanours.

76 *The Front* (1976): Directed by Martin Ritt, starring Woody Allen and Zero Mostel. Yet another study of the McCarthy era, Allen plays a restaurant cashier who serves as a 'front' for blacklisted scriptwriters. Humorous and based on the director's own experiences.

77 *Skokie* (1981): A made for TV dramatization of the famous case (discussed in chapter 2). Herbert Wise directs, Danny Kaye stars.

78 *Dirty Pictures* (2000): In 1990, Dennis Barrie, director of the Cincinnati Contemporary Arts Centre, focuses on the 1990 trial of Cincinnati Contemporary Arts Center director Dennis Barrie, who was accused of promoting pornography by presenting an exhibit of photographs by Robert Mapplethorpe. These included images of naked children and graphic displays of homosexual sadomasochism. Barrie was eventually acquitted. The movie is a dramatisation of the case. Directed by Frank Pierson.

79 *Good Night, and Good Luck* (2005): Another treatment of the McCarthy witch-hunts. Broadcasting journalist Ed Murrow (David Strathairn) and his producer Fred Friendly (George Clooney) set out to challenge and expose McCarthy. Clooney directs.

80 *The Live of Others* (2007): Florian Henckel von Donnersmarck's gripping study of the STASI at work. Agent Gerd Wiesler (Ulrich Mühe) becomes increasingly fascinated by the lives of those he is paid to spy upon.

81 *Manuscripts Don't Burn* (2013): Director Mohammad Rasoulof. This film featured at the Cannes film festival, where it received a standing ovation. It was made in secret and had to be smuggled out of Iran. It is based on the real-life story of 21 Iranian writers and academics travelling on a bus who survived a botched attempt on their lives. Rasoulof had already served time in Iran for 'actions and propaganda against the system' after trying to make a documentary about the unrest that followed the disputed re-election of President Mahmoud Ahmadinejad in 2009.

9 organizations/websites devoted to the cause of free speech

The self-descriptions are drawn from the relevant websites.

82 Index on Censorship: www.indexoncensorship.org, 'an international organisation that promotes and defends the right to freedom of expression'.

83 Hacked Off: http://hackinginquiry.org 'the campaign for a free and accountable press'.

84 Free Speech Debate: http://freespeechdebate.com Inspired and organized by Oxford's Timothy Garton Ash, the website offers the chance to participate in a 'global conversation' about free expression.

85 Committee to Protect Journalists: http://www.cpj.org/ Supports journalists who risk murder or imprisonment merely for doing their job.

86 Article 19: http://www.article19.org/ So named after article 19 of the UN Declaration of Universal Human Rights, the organization 'works worldwide to combat freedom of expression and information'.

87 Electronic Frontier Foundation: https://www.eff.org/ 'The leading non-profit organization defending civil liberties in the digital world'.

88 IFEX (formerly the International Freedom of Expression Exchange). https://www.ifex.org/ A 'network of organisations ...' connected by a shared commitment to defend and promote freedom of expression as a fundamental human right'.

89 Amnesty International campaigns 'on behalf of thousands of prisoners of conscience – people who are imprisoned because of their political, religious or other conscientiously held beliefs, ethnic origin, sex, colour, language, national or social origin, economic status, birth, sexual orientation or other status'. See http://www.amnesty.org/en/freedom-of-expression There is an annual Amnesty 'freedom of expression award' for 'an outstanding play at the Edinburgh Festival carrying a human rights message'.

90 No Hate Speech Movement: http://www.nohatespeechmovement.org/, 'A youth campaign of the

Council of Europe for human rights online, to reduce the
levels of acceptance of hate speech and to develop online
youth participation'.

10 literary classics which have been subject to censorship in the past

91 James Joyce: *Ulysses*

92 Mark Twain: *The Adventures of Huckleberry Finn*

93 Gustave Flaubert: *Madame Bovary*

94 Nathaniel Hawthorne: *The Scarlet Letter*

95 Harriet Beecher Stowe: *Uncle Tom's Cabin*

96 John Steinbeck: *Of Mice and Men*

97 Aldous Huxley: *Brave New World*

98 D.H.Lawrence: *Lady Chatterley's Lover*

99 Daniel Defoe: *Moll Flanders*

100 Voltaire: *Candide*

100 Ideas

Texts cited

In the course of my discussion, I have referred to the following texts. Where I have included quotations, their source should be clear enough. However, I have done without footnotes, so there are no precise text and page references.

Ackerman, Bruce & Fishkin, James 'Deliberation Day', in Fishkin, James S & Laslett, Peter eds (2003) *Debating Deliberative Democracy*, Oxford: Blackwell

Ashton, Doré (1972) *Picasso on Art: A Selection of Views*, New York: Da Capo Press

Augustine, *A Treatise Concerning the Correction of the Donatists* or *Epistle CLXXXV*: http://www.tertullian.org/fathers2/NPNF1-04/npnf1-04-63.htmref.

Cohen, Nick (2012) *You Can't Read This Book: Censorship in an Age of Freedom*, Harper Collins

Dahl, Robert A. (1956) *A Preface to Democratic Theory*, Cgucago: University of Chicago Press. Kindle Edition.

Dworkin, Ronald, 'The Right to Ridicule' *New York Review of Books*, 23/03/2006

Evans, Richard J. (2002) *Telling Lies About Hitler: Holocaust, History, and the David Irving Trial*, London & New York: Verso

Finlayson, James Gordon (2005) *Habermas: A Very Short Introduction*, Oxford: Oxford University Press

Garton Ash, Timothy (2010) *Facts are Subversive: Political Writing from a Decade without a Name*, Atlantic Books

Gutmann, Amy & Thompson, Dennis (1996) *Democracy and Disagreement*, Harvard: Belknap Press

Gutmann, Amy & Thomson, Dennis (2002) 'Deliberative Democracy Beyond Process' in Fishkin James, S & Laslett, Peter, eds (2003) *Debating Deliberative Democracy*, Oxford: Blackwell

Jürgen Habermas (1989) *The Structural Transformation of the Public Sphere*, Oxford: Blackwell

David Hume (1953) [1714] 'Of the Liberty of the Press' in Charles W.Hendel. ed., *David Hume's Political Essays*, Indianapolis: Bobbs-Merrill

Koonz, Claudia (2003) *The Nazi Conscience*, Harvard: Belknap Press, pp. 5–6

Lipstadt, Deborah (1994) *Denying the Holocaust: The Growing Assault on Truth and Memory*, London: Penguin, and Evans

Madison, *Federalist* 47, in Hamilton, Alexander; Jay, John; Madison, James (1987) [1788] *The Federalist Papers* , London: Penguin

Marcuse, Herbert (1969) 'Repressive Tolerance', in Wolff, Robert Paul, Moore Jnr, Barrington, and Marcuse, Herbert, *A Critique of Pure Tolerance*, London: Jonathan Cape

Meiklejohn, Alexander (1948) *Free Speech and its Relation to Self-Government*, New York: Harper and

Brothers, available at http://digital.library.wisc.edu/ 1711.dl/UW.MeikFreeSp (Why is this important text only accessible via the website of the University of Wisconsin collection?)

Mill, John Stuart (1828) 'Law of Libel and the Liberty of the Press' in Geraint L.Williams, ed. (1976): *John Stuart Mill on Politics and Society,* London: Fontana

Mill, John Stuart (1832) 'The Spirit of the Age' in Geraint L.Williams, ed. (1976): *John Stuart Mill on Politics and Society,* London: Fontana

Mill, John Stuart (1859) *On Liberty* (There are so many editions of Mill's famous essay that it would be ridiculous to cite any particular one.)

Milton, John [1644] *Areopagitica*, in C.A.Patrides, ed.,(1974) *John Milton: Selected Prose*, London: Penguin, pp.196–248

Neier, Aryeh (1979 & 2012) *Defending my Enemy: American Nazis, the Skokie Case, and the Risks of Freedom*, New York, London, and Amsterdam, International Debate Education Association

OK, Issue 909, December 17, 2013. p. 33

Plato (1987) [*circa* 375BCE] *The Republic*, trans Desmond Lee, London: Penguin

Rawls, John (1993) *Political Liberalism*, New York: Columbia University Press

Rousseau, Jean Jacques (1968) [1762] *The Social Contract*, London : Penguin, p.153

Rushdie, Salman (1990) 'Is Nothing Sacred?' (Herbert Read memorial Lecture) Cambridge, Granta

Rushdie, Salman, interviewed in *The Hindu*, 08/10/2012

Rushdie, Salman (2013), *Joseph Anton*, London, Vintage

Scanlon, T.M. (1972) 'A Theory of Freedom of Expression', in Scanlon.T.M.(2003) *The Difficulty of Tolerance*, Cambridge: Cambridge University Press

Schumpeter, Joseph (1943) *Capitalism, Socialism, and Democracy*, London: Unwin

de Tocqueville, Alexis (2003) [1835 & 1840] *Democracy in America*, London: Penguin

Waldron, Jeremy (2012) *The Harm in Hate Speech*, Cambridge Mass. & London England, Harvard University Press